SWEATY EQUITY

A BALL BOY, A BILLIONAIRE, AND THE
BONKERS STARTUP TALE YOU'VE NEVER HEARD

MIKE SHANNON

ODD DRAFT PRESS

An imprint of Odd Draft Press, LLC
Chicago, Illinois

First edition July 2025

Manufactured in the United States of America

1 3 5 7 9 10 8 6 4 2

Interior design by Opeyemi Ikuborije
Cover illustration by Kostis Pavlou
Cover photo credited to Sara Wert

Sweaty Equity: A Ball Boy, A Billionaire, and the Bonkers
Startup Tale You've Never Heard / by Mike Shannon.
— First edition.

Identifiers:
ISBN 979-8-9988920-0-4 (Paperback)
ISBN 979-8-9988920-1-1 (eBook)

Subjects:
Entrepreneurship — Biography.
Startups — Personal narratives.
Basketball — Anecdotes.
Business storytelling.
Humor.

For Mom, who gave us the paint brush, and Dad, who installed the hustle.

For my ride-or-die siblings, Amy, Patti, Kelly, and Danny.

For Morgan, Logan, and Miles.

Written in loving memory of Kevin D'Agostino, a hero who engaged all challenges head on, and never bothered to control his pattern of speech.

CONTENTS

Author's Disclaimer

As with life, this book may well be taken as a comedy. No hard feelings.

That said, while some names have been changed, and many anecdotes were sacrificed to the editing process, all events of this story occurred truthfully as described.

Chapter 1

Don't F*ck
the Shaman

January 19, 2013. Chicago, Illinois.

It was an odd start to what should have been considered a strange week.

On Tuesday, I'd interact with a stark-naked Kobe Bryant, north of midnight, part of a search team on a quest to find him a post-game cocktail. That was after Kobe spent an hour and a half sitting silently in the tiny broom closet at the back corner of the visitor's locker room with a Gatorade towel draped over his head. My Bulls had whooped his Lakers.

On Thursday, I'd engage a locker-side self-introduction to an NBA player who would, before year's end and unbeknownst to my bosses, wire an investment to me. I suppose that hushed elevator pitch was a harbinger on how my two worlds were destined to collide.

Entrepreneur by day.

NBA Ball Boy by night.

At this point, neither my friend Kasey nor I had ever seen an angel check. I probably should've been spending the weekend applying for a real job. Kasey probably should've been doing his homework before getting back to class on Monday.

But instead, we hopped the elevator of the lakeside luxury high rise to the forty-eighth floor, and stepped foot inside the home of a mysterious stranger.

"You motherfucker!" hollered one commodities trader to the other, before punching him square in the face.

The story at hand was a defining piece of our sixty-year-old host's nostalgic recollection of his beloved 1970s era Chicago Board of Trade. His pitch-black ponytail had silver roots. The aroma of church-like incense filled his living room. A little white paper structure rolled up into a stick rested on his ear as he leaned forward in his wooden rocking chair.

"Just fuckin' punched him in the face," recalled Alan Matthew, "right in the *fuckin'* face!"

It was the latest conversational detour down a rabbit hole that originated, I think, with an ordinary small talk question about how his career began. Which is to say, where he got his bag of money that we were now vying for.

"I thought, *fuuuck*, this is for me." concluded Alan, his face cracking into a wry smile, "Hehehe."

He didn't laugh much throughout our meeting, but when he did, it had a peculiar sort of dryness to it. Not as dry, of course, as the industry we were plotting to crack into with the help of his dough.

College textbooks.

Because, as goes the cliché, college student entrepreneurs tend to chase after college student problems. The textbook represented, in those days, everybody's least favorite two-hundred-dollar pain in the ass. So, in a fashion shared with every other Steve-Jobs-Biography-Reading wantrepreneur of the era, we made it our God-blessed mission to *disrupt* textbooks.

PackbackBooks.com would, according to the Illinois State University Business Plan Competition that we'd won about a year earlier, *revolutionize* higher education by providing "pay per use" access to textbook content in the form of 24-hour digital rentals. Just five bucks a day.

Much to the horror of anti-cramming academics nationwide.

By now, we even had a Letter of Intent (LOI) signed by the top dogs at one of the Big Three educational publishers. That's a funny little story involving a big silly guy, but we'll get to it later. Anyways, LOI in hand, all we needed — as far as my naivety could tell — was a little cash to get the platform off the ground, and then we'd be soaring.

Alan Matthew also knew a thing or two about getting high.

Back when his trading career began, his legal name was Alan Matthew Sooley. A good Catholic kid, like me, who'd at that point spent more time serving as an altar boy than perusing the desert of Burning Man. But Alan always wondered. Always wrote down the contents of his dreams. Those dreams influenced life decisions. Guided trades. And eventually, shaped his identity.

Years into his career, it was during a dream that he saw a billboard which read "Alan Matthew Clothing." The clothing part didn't much matter. It was the name that spoke to him. Alan Sooley died that day.

Alan Matthew was born.

And Alan Matthew traveled further down the road of the irregular.

His daily attire while moving markets on the trading floor was a custom design bespeckled vest, worn under his signature black ponytail. He routinely commuted through the camps of Burning Man in a fluffy pink motorized bunny. Experimented with mind-bending substances. Chief among them was a plant-based psychedelic called ayahuasca, a strong hallucinogenic integrated into the rituals that he took part in throughout recurring visits to the Peruvian Amazon. It was down there in the Amazon that Alan found his new tribe:

The Shamans.

Before long, Alan was adopted as a "gringo Shaman" himself.

Like the market waves he rode, by the time Kasey and I plopped down on the snow leopard white couch in his living room, Alan Matthew had been up, down, and all around the world.

New to my twenties, I'd barely ever left the state of Illinois.

New to his sixties, Alan had officially left the trading pit.

Reborn yet again, his new game was that of angel investing in startup companies. And like everything else he'd done in life, Alan Matthew dove in headfirst.

But the DNA lurking beneath the surface of his bubbly-looking new playground was as strange to Alan as Alan was to us. He soon encountered problems with the startup world. Problems that aggravated him deeply.

The trading floor had been a ruthless pit; a blunt society defined by "fuck you" greetings amongst rivals and the cold-hearted honesty of market numbers. Whether somebody was up or down, everybody else knew it. When the tribe had a problem with a member, they circled up and dealt with the bad actor amongst themselves. That world was cold. Vile. And yet, most critically to Alan Matthew, it was transparent.

The startup world was different.

Cocktail networking hours humming with vaguely specific founder tales of "crushing it." Illustrious pitch decks. Smiles & rah-rahs. The fog of its niceties rendered an undecipherable, or at times, unenforceable code of integrity in Chicago's nascent startup scene that revered Silicon Valley like a cool older cousin.

Void of a dependable jungle code, Alan Matthew was exposed to be duped as an angel investor. As such, he amassed a growing list of foes.

Chief among them was an entrepreneur in whom Alan had invested a hundred grand to build some sort of game. As the story went, the thing was built, and it worked. And then, for unspecified reasons, the guy decided to shut it down. Alan's money was lost. Sometime later, Alan saw the guy on a corner in Chicago standing outside of a nice restaurant. He had his phone out. Alan asked him what he was doing. He was ordering a premium Uber Black for his girlfriend.

"…with *my* fucking money!" Alan hollered at us.

More stories. More emotions. Alan ran himself through an exhausting series of mental rollercoasters as he retold his tales. It wasn't just the entrepreneurs who'd wronged him, it was also the nature of the terms gained by the venture capitalists who put their money in after his. And in the sting of his scar tissue, our conversation had a way of returning to a single point of orbit:

Alan's desire, if he were to invest in us, for *non-dilutable* shares.

When our dialogue with Alan began months earlier, spawned of a cold call and subsequent email thread as Kasey and I sat inside of Chicago's new tech coworking space and Alan trotted around somewhere in Hawaii, I'd asked a friendly-uncle-type advisor of ours about this peculiar request for "non-dilutable" shares.

It was a phrase I wasn't familiar with.

The advisor, an old dog venture capitalist named Sam Guren, whose tales included the early investment he'd made for his firm in a startup company called "Apple Computers," had his own phrase for classifying Alan's request.

"Look guys," explained Sam, "that's what I call an NFW."

No Fucking Way.

As such, we were rendered stuck between a rock and a hard place, still void of our first angel check and unable to accept the terms of the guy closest to writing one.

"So," I began, in my latest attempt to veer the conversation away from Alan's scarred memories, "Your assistant pointed out a few concerns she had with our competitors, mainly Chegg and CourseSmart. Did you get a chance to look at the competitor analysis summary I sent over?"

His assistant was, as far as I could gather from Alan's description, the "former hairdresser or something" who now ran due diligence on his angel investment pipeline.

"Yea, uh, I saw that she sent it over to me," acknowledged Alan, "but no, I didn't actually read it."

"Ok, well basically…"

Kasey and I proceeded to ed-tech jargon-talk our way through explanations of how our yet-to-exist company will victoriously compete in a market that neither of us had ever worked in.

…Chegg only offers semester-long physical book rentals, so there's still a frequency of use issue, let alone a "combative" relationship with publishers!

…CourseSmart's model runs counter to financial and academic freedom for students!

It was all fascinating stuff, which all bored the hell out of Alan.

Fatigued of our joint lecture, he broke his blank stare and cut us off with a simple question:

"So how do you make money?"

How do we make money?

We'd just long-windedly showcased our vast knowledge about textbook cost issues, the "cannibalization" of publisher revenue due to the used book market, and the God-forsaken "lagging digital adoption rate" of course materials in higher education!

Was he not impressed?!

What a dumb question.

How could he – wait, how exactly do we make money again?

"Uh, wh-what do you mean?" I asked.

"How do you make *money!* How do you pay the bills?!"

"Ohhh." I recovered, "Like how are we personally paying bills right now?"

Wait till this dude hears about the thirty-five bucks per game I rake in as a Chicago Bulls Ball Boy while living at home with my parents.

"Nooo!" hollered Alan across the living room coffee table. "The company! How does the company make money?!"

With all our hoopla about the grand injustice of "eight hundred and twelve percent textbook price inflation," we'd put the explanation of our own revenue model aside. Investors apparently don't like it when you do that.

Kasey took this one.

As my partner rambled on about the conservative nature of our bombastically delusional projected pro forma financials, I whipped out a laptop and handed Alan a view at the three-year forecast that Kasey was verbalizing.

Alan wasn't interested in studying a spreadsheet.

"Ok, so you still haven't answered my question," he said, nearing another frustration boil-over, "how do you *make money??*"

A shared pause.

"Well," I said, "we make money when students rent the book. About half will convert into semester-long purchases while the other half sticks to daily rental. Revenue is split 70/30 in favor of publishers."

Apparently satisfied, Alan's mind bounced elsewhere.

"You know, there used to be these things called payphone stations that you'd go to make calls. Kids would take these little recorder devices to the machine, hold it up to the dial, it'd go *clink* and they'd make the calls for free," Alan explained with an air of firsthand experience. "A savvy coder is going to rip your books and get everything for free. What's stopping him?"

Kasey jumped on it.

"Yes, so this is exactly the reason we're going with a third-party E-Reader, Adobe Digital Editions, which has all the protective 'digital rights management' software in place to prevent this from happening."

Satisfactory.

We continued.

I made the mistake of wandering into an illustrious explanation of our ideated "phase two" in which Packback would one day push next-gen digital products straight to students on behalf of publishers.

Alan took an interest in that.

"So how do you know when to push a certain product?" he asked.

Why, I'm so glad you asked!

"Ok," I proudly replied, "so for example, if thirty kids are spending an additional average time on a given three-pages, we'll know that—based on past learning habits—'X program' probably would adhere best to getting the student through this slump."

It was a confusing and unproven thing to explain.

Alan was appropriately unimpressed.

"Last week I was reading this thing," he explained, "went to go, I don't know, take a shit or something, and left the thing open."

Silence.

He said nothing more.

Was that ...a question?

"Uhh, yea" replied Kasey, "there are ways around problems like that. But anyways the basic concepts are there."

For two tumultuous hours, our conversation bounced onward with the linearity of a pinball bum rushing an octagon of bumpers. I could never quite predict where Alan's mind would land next.

Back to the Amazon jungle.

While providing a verbal tutorial of the hallucinogenic effects of ayahuasca, Alan paused periodically when gathering his thoughts or finding the right words. The pause was often accompanied by a piercing stare. Sometimes that stare was aimed off into the distance.

This time it was aimed directly at Kasey.

"...I can go inside of your head," Alan explained to Kasey amidst a prolonged stretch of eye contact.

He wasn't joking, and he didn't mean it as a figure of speech.

"...but I wouldn't do that." He concluded.

Phew!

Back to startup investments.

Conniving entrepreneurs aside, it was the dilution of deals past that had scarred Alan above all. He mumbled illegibly through a moment or two while grasping for the apt vocabulary to portray the nuance of his woes.

Then he annunciated:

"I'm getting fucked," he declared, "I mean *fuuucked!* Just ...FUCKED!"

Like coal to a locomotive, the word "fuck" had the peculiar effect of fueling an escalation in Alan's volume. It was a self-reinforcing pump, unleashing from Alan the animated reenactment of whichever memory our pinball landed on next.

Once again, his eyes locked in on Kasey, who, in the theatre of Alan's mind, had been volunteered to play the role of Alan's counterpart in a reenacted dialogue. I can't recall what the story was. What I remember is the gesture that it revolved around.

Alan stared into Kasey's eyes.

His finger was soon fully outstretched, pointing upwards. Not the index finger. It was the bad finger. The one most favored by Catholic school fifth graders worldwide.

The *middle* one.

His story progressed.

A scoop of F-grade coal was poured into the locomotive engine as his volume increased on cue.

"Fuck you. ...*Fuck* you! ....*FUUUUCK! YOUUUU!*" hollered Alan as our sixty-year-old middle-finger-pointing pony-tailed host leaned toward Kasey from the edge of his wooden rocking chair.

It was just a story. A role play. Alan's rage was not actually intended for us, but the reenactment of it carried a not-so-subliminal message:

If, by some miracle, we land his investment, we could be the next recipient of this rage if any crack in trust occurs.

But that was an irrelevant concern, because our meeting was hitting a brick wall. A month ago, we'd had the investment in the bag. Now it was slipping away.

Back to the crux of all that pained Alan Matthew:

Dilution.

"I'm just getting stepped on constantly," he said, "I come in early, then the next guy steps on me. Then I get buried by whatever venture comes in. I'm getting *fucked!*"

It's a conversational loop that we can't get past.

Alan wants non-dilutable shares. We can't give them to him.

Our drunken obstacle course of a meeting had devolved from far-left field to straight downhill. We didn't need any more time. We needed a conclusion.

I heaved up a final attempt at reigning Alan back into the elegant "less than attorneys, more than a napkin" agreement we'd reached over email.

"Look," I began, "you said it exactly, there are a million ideas out there. It comes down to who can execute..."

Words as a brush, I painted away: our gritty student-entrepreneur origin story, rich with the type of hustle-hard antics that eventually landed us that cease-and-desist letter from our own campus bookstore. The cold call to the white whale. The offshore dev shop accelerator we'd been accepted into after writing our own letter of recommendation and asking a nice guy named Mark Achler to sign it. The market research firm that agreed to lend us their extra cubicle space and conduct a few focus groups as part of a makeshift "incubator" that we'd concocted after being denied, again, by Tech Stars. The meetings we had lined up with local big dogs, none bigger than the man dubbed the "Wizard of Chicago Tech" whom Alan respected most: Howard Tullman.

And of course, the *eight billion dollar* textbook market opportunity ripe for disruption.

When my desperate stump speech finally ended, there was silence.

Alan became contemplative. Kasey and I held our tongues as we stared across the living room at a man who'd sailed the winds of the financial markets, walked the desert of Burning Man, and drank from the elixir of Peruvian Shamans before either of us were ever born.

Make him speak next.

"So," asked Alan, still contemplating, "what's the deal again?"

"Fifteen 'K' for one and a half percent" I replied.

Alan stood up from the rocking chair. Without a word, he turned around, walked past the wall of sacred woodwork he'd imported from China, said nothing to that stone statue of a goddess riding a lion, turned left across from the indoor waterfall structure that trickled endlessly in the background, and disappeared down a hallway.

Icy Lake Michigan glistened outside the wall-sized windows of the high-rise condo as Kasey and I sat frozen in silence on the snow leopard white couch.

Principal's office vibes. A feeling I'd known well as a child.

We made eye contact. A dangerous move, as each of us desperately tried not to let the confused half smile on our face crack any further. *Knock it off!* I told myself, aware that the release of a tiny chuckle could trigger a volcanic eruption of nervous laughter. The afternoon had progressed from slightly unusual to fully strange. And now we were forty-some-odd floors above ground, suspended in the cliffhanger of the moment.

Then Alan Matthew returned.

There was something in his hand, small & rectangular. A checkbook. He placed it on the coffee table and began writing.

Another glance of eye contact between Kasey and me. Another tongue-bite to maintain poker faces.

"Who do I make the check out to?" asked Alan.

Good question! Hell if I knew.

"Umm. Packback." I improvised, "Yea just make it out to Packback."

Kasey agreed. *Duh.* Alan continued writing.

When finished, he ripped the check from the checkbook and tossed it on the coffee table.

"Here," said Alan, "don't fuck it up."

Don't fuck it up.

And with those holy words of the Shaman's blessing, our meeting was adjourned. Void of a legal document or so much as a droplet of ink on a napkin in sight, I held in my hand a fifteen-thousand-dollar check.

Without a fool's clue as to how badly we were in fact going to fuck it up.

As we stood for the exit, another entrepreneur entered. Alan introduced us, and like a wind-up doll, the man snapped into a succinctly polished elevator pitch about how he was on the verge of disrupting Facebook.

It was his turn at the altar.

Kasey and I rode down the elevator without speaking a word. *Keep a straight face; anyone may be watching.* We waved goodbye to the suit clad man at the front desk, departed the lobby door, continued walking down the sidewalk a bit, and then, finally, we exhaled.

Holy shit dude!

I handed the check to Kasey.

We both had the same question: what do we do with this thing?

Do we wait for a contract? How do start-up investments work anyways? Should we just …deposit it? A mystery for tomorrow. For now, Kasey had to get back down to Illinois State before class on Monday, and I had to catch a cab.

My other hat called for duty.

Shuffling into the back seat of the cab, I delivered my two-word instructions:

"United Center."

The Memphis Grizzlies were in town.

Chapter 2

The Ten Commandments of the Ball Boys

Smack. Whistle. Grunt. Plop.

Down went Ben Wallace.

I grabbed the mop and sprinted out onto the court.

I'm starting to get the hang of this.

Or so I thought.

Wait, huh?

What the hell?

It was a factor I hadn't yet encountered in my several game experience on mop duty. The six-foot-nine, two-hundred-forty-pound afro-rockin' four-time NBA Defensive Player of the Year was on his back, looking up at me as I arrived with my mop.

Then he did the unexpected.

Under the bright lights of a stadium packed with twenty thousand fans and countless cameras watching us, he reached his right arm out towards me.

Big Ben needed a hand getting back on his feet.

With the mop in my left, I locked right hands with Wallace.

Tug.

Tug!

Tug harder! Everyone is watching goddammit!

It was no use; I wasn't strong enough. The glistening block of muscle marble in my hand wouldn't budge.

Within seconds, two Bulls players came to the rescue and pulled Wallace up from the ground. He left behind a pond of sweat.

No worries, folks. I got this.

Just another day at the office.

Of the misconceptions that arise when you tell somebody that you were "a *ball boy* for the Bulls," the predominant act of naivety is their assumption that this was something you did as a child. You know, when you were a *boy*.

And yea, there were always a few of those rookies shuffling in and out, typically being a kid with some family ties to the organization.

But the purest of our kind, whose qualifications might otherwise have landed them behind the register of a hotdog stand up in the nosebleeds, would roll out of bed, shave the beard, shake off a hangover, count their untaxed cash, and at some point around midafternoon they'd pull up their ball boy sweatpants, flash an all-access badge at security, and get back to it.

Ball Boy Land was an enterprise of grown men.

The structure under which we operated could make for a compelling management case study.

We officially reported to the assistant trainer, but served any number of stakeholders across the trainers, equipment manager, coaches, players, and whoever else caught the impulse to ask you to go fetch something for them.

The assistant trainer, of course, had his own career to worry about. He hadn't earned multiple degrees in studying the anatomy of elite athletes so that he could one day "manage" a raggedy bullpen of ball boys. His job was to keep the mega millions of dollars that the Chicago Bulls Organization spent on player payroll healthy. Overseeing our existence was just some random extra thing that had been tossed onto his plate.

Hence, Ball Boy Land was effectively ruled by the vets.

And since the trainers were busy in the trainers room, and the ball boy duties occurred everywhere else, the bulk of our work went unseen by the bosses. Our manager's perception of what was happening thus relied on informal reports from the locker room vets who might occasionally share their observations.

Those were, of course, the same vets who were keen on protecting their territory from any and all newcomer turf threats.

So, you figured out how to work hard, but not in such a manner that threatened the vets, and if you were lucky you gained favor with a vet who might share a good word about you with the bosses. That's how, as a part-timer like me, you wiggled your way into the regular rotation.

Now, I don't mean to imply that there was no formality to our governance.

We had doctrine all right.

Governing the behaviors of a ball boy was an official list of phrases. They existed, for a period, on a piece of printer paper Scotch-taped to a wall in the players' lounge of the Bulls locker room. Conveniently eye-level right at the spot where Bulls equipment manager, "Ligs," used to plop down the overstuffed bin of Gatorade towels that were to be folded upon our arrival.

Consider these the Ten Commandments of the Ball Boys:

Chicago Bulls Ball Boys
HOW WE OPERATE

1. BE PROFESSIONAL
2. CONTROL YOUR PATTERN OF SPEECH
3. DEVELOP A HIGH LEVEL
OF CONCENTRATION
4. PLAYERS COME FIRST
5. DEVELOP AND MAINTAIN A SENSE
OF URGENCY
6. BE ON TIME
7. CONTROL YOUR EMOTIONS;
HANDLE PRESSURE
8. DEVELOP A SENSE OF APPRECIATION FOR
WHERE YOU ARE
9. TREAT PEOPLE WITH RESPECT
10. DEVELOP YOUR ABILITY TO LISTEN

Behavioral Commandments established, a list of Fourteen Rules was later published. Much like the Commandments, it was unclear which events of history had inspired each one. Take, for example, Rules Number Nine and Ten:

9. No eating food on the court or any area of the floor.

10. Only eat food that is provided to you by the media lounge, or food you have purchased from the concession stand.

I couldn't tell you what had transpired to justify dedicating two whole rules to our food consumption habits. Nor do I claim an educated guess at what odd scene had once unfolded that made it necessary to specify, in Rule Number Seven, that the ball boys *should not* "practice with players during warmups."

All I know is that the rules were the rules.

And at the end of this Rules document was a phrase that formalized our standing on the organizational totem pole, which is to say, clarified our dispensable place at the bottom of it:

Being a Chicago Bulls Ballboy is a PRIVILEGE. Keep in mind that as a Chicago Bulls Ballboy, you are representing the Chicago Bulls Organization, the Team, the Players, yourself and your family. Please present yourself professionally in all situations.

The privilege bit was no lie; we were each insanely lucky to be there. A die-hard Bulls fan myself, I can tell you with certainty that taking a single day's stroll through our reality would surpass any Bulls fan's wildest dream. Quite obviously, it would be easy to replace any one of us.

Which made climbing the ranks a precarious game to play.

On the foundation of our Commandments and our Rules, a third resource detailing the "Ballboy Duties" was eventually published as well, outlining *thirty-seven* duties in all. Those duties entailed doing stuff like bringing basketballs out to the court, pre-game rebounding until no players remained on the court, washing & wiping down coolers and Gatorade carts, hanging up laundry after the game, so on and so forth.

You get the picture.

We did the *stuff*.

At the end of the night, we were handed a white envelope containing anywhere between twenty-five and thirty-five bucks cash, depending on your tenure. For the most of us, that was the money we made. But the seniormost vets, in the sanctuary of their coveted locker room turf, trafficked in a far more lucrative, unspoken enterprise of player favors.

At that, one prevailed above all.

On my first day as a ball boy, upon entering through a mysterious *Gate Three-and-a-Half* and making it past security on the coattails of a remarkably confident twelve-year ball boy that the Bulls had apparently just picked up off the waivers from the Phoenix Suns,[1] I stepped unchecked through the front door of the Bulls locker room. After saying hello to a player named Tyrus Thomas who was getting dressed at

---

1. I had the appearance of an eighteen-year-old going on twelve, was dressed in raggedy sweatpants, and lacked the necessary ID badge as I stood at the check-in table nervously attempting to explain myself to the suit clad United Center security staff. That's when, like a savior from the sky, a tall, handsome, stylishly dressed grown man walked up behind me.

"I'm the same as him" he told the security guards.

That can't be right, I thought. This tall handsome man was easily pushing mid-twenties.

"We're ball boys," he said, "they should have our names on the list, since we haven't gotten our IDs."

"Alright alright," replied the security guard, softened by my savior's impeccable confidence, "what's yer names?"

As the guards conversed on their radios and, to my amazement, scribbled out all-access VIP guest passes for us, I introduced myself to my new hero.

"Hey, I'm Mike." I said, "So, uh, where do you go to school?"

"Aaron." he replied. "I graduated from Arizona State, now going to grad school in Chicago. I was with the Suns for twelve years."

Did he say, twelve?

Twelve years ago, I was blissfully enrolled as a kindergartener. This guy was gainfully employed as a…?

"As a *ball boy*?" I asked.

"No as a point guard." He snarked, "Yea as a ball boy."

A tenure of that degree ranked him among the worldliest men I'd ever met in my young life.

Impressively experienced though he was, after our first game together I never saw Aaron again. It's safe to assume what happened to him. Capable of sniffing out a turf threat a mile away, the vets chewed him up like a pack of wolves in their informal reviews to our bosses.

Welcome to Chicago, pal.

Better luck in grad school.

his locker, my new colleague and I ventured down another hallway and soon arrived in a leather chair-filled back room called the players' lounge.

That was where, after meeting our boss, assistant trainer Marc Boff, a welcoming speech and tour was provided by a vet named Kevin D'Agostino.

Having never considered that a change of clothes might be possible, I'd arrived to my first day of work at the organization that I cherished more than anything in the world, dressed like an orphan at gym class.

"So, Shannon," said Kevin, eying me up and down, "you really dressed up for work, huh?"

"Ha, yea, well, uh," I stumbled into a shy, embarrassed reply, "I figured you guys wear sweatpants, so I just thought—"

"Yea yea, whatever, it's cool," said Kevin, "nobody gives a shit. Let alone knows you exist here."

Kevin and I had some familiarity. Growing up, I'd marveled at "Kevin D" as an older kid at the same small Catholic grade school as me. It was through two others grade school friends, Brendan Ryan and Pat Reardon, whom Kevin had *actually* invited to a tryout to become ball boys, that I wound up being accidentally hired instead.

Kevin D'Agostino was a different sort of vet.

He was twig-thin, barely taller than me, and yet he had a bellowing voice, distinctly low with a raspy touch. He was good looking. Engaging. Funny. In the years to come, I'd witness Kevin talk shop with sportscasters in the media cafeteria, hurl paper Gatorade cups at fellow ball boys during timeouts, make a seven-foot rookie player blush by celebrating the guy's first double-double, and receive-then-decline the invitation to sit on the trainer's table for a post-game beer with starting point guard, Kirk Heinrich.

For years after he graduated, his high school wrestling coach told stories of Kevin D'Agostino being one of the toughest kids he'd ever coached.

That was despite Kevin's bad cough, which occasionally morphed into a full coughing fit, like you might expect from a heavy smoker. Except Kevin didn't smoke cigarettes. Kevin suffered from cystic fibrosis, a rare and, as of this writing, uncurable lung disease that rendered its victims to an expected lifespan not much older than Kevin.

By medical prognosis, Kevin was on borrowed time. Whether or not that was the reason why, he lived and engaged his life with a vibrance as such. He'd go on to become a nurse and serve a tour on the United States medical staff in Afghanistan. It would not be cliché to say that Kevin D'Agostino would give a stranger the shirt off his back, no questions asked.

But not before landing a zinger.

Nobody was off the hook from Kevin's quick-witted tongue.

"So, who have you met?" asked Kevin. "Have you seen Flounder?"

"No, who's that?" I replied.

Or what is that?

Ring went the bell as class began on my Education as a Ball Boy.

"Ok, there's gonna be two fatasses you'll see around here," explained Kevin. "They work the Bulls locker room. One of them is black, the other white. The black one, Sharrod, he's real cool, very nice guy. He won't bother you. The white fatass, Flounder, well, his real name is Nate, but everyone around here calls him Flounder because he looks like a fat fuckin' fish. He's Luol Deng's and Ben Gordon's personal bitch..."

That was how I came to know of the man they called Flounder.

And, placing aside our Ten Commandments, Fourteen Rules, and Thirty-Seven Duties, it's a glance at Flounder – a Ball Boy career of the highest degree – that provides the most fitting portrait of Ball Boy Land.

Namely, a glimpse at its most complex, shadowy element: Turf.

If ever there was a policy written up for determining ball boy turf allocation, I couldn't tell you what it said. Never saw it. What I can explain is this:

Ball boy turf wasn't so much earned as it was *squatted upon*.

To advance your station in ball boy life was to play a game of chicken.

When the unexpected moment of locker room turf availability arrived, you had to be willing to *not* jump at the actual necessary task – namely, going out to the court to rebound – and rather loiter inside the locker room long enough to be pegged to run an errand for a player.

When might that spot open up, you ask?

Well, answering that question would require an estimate of the retirement timeline of a locker room vet, which is a complicated and frankly inappropriate question for you to be asking.

By definition, a ball boy was *supposed* to be an actively enrolled student, but let's just keep that between you and me. Nevertheless, the career of any given ball boy was, in essence, a Cinderella story. Not because of his remarkably enchanted behind-the-scenes NBA surroundings, but rather due to the condition of his tale's predestined conclusion.

In the ordinary workplace, as years racked up, you'd be a *tenured employee.*

In Ball Boy Land, as years racked up, you'd be *getting away with something.*

Eventually, the clock struck midnight on every ball boy's career, and his carriage turned to a pumpkin.

End of fairy tale.

Fair enough, I suppose. Not unlike the players, who were said to be grown adults playing a child's game, we were grown men working a boy's gig. But destiny be damned, the savviest of vets employed a mindset that defied the somber gravity of birth certificates and verified student IDs.

Forget Cinderella.

I'm Peter Pan, motherfuckers.

Thus, the unwritten ball boy hierarchy cemented itself as the immovable full-time locker room vets creeped closer and closer to their thirties. As their decade-tenure mark came and went, the seniormost vets arguably weren't even interested in our privilege anymore. They'd grown numb to it.

I once observed a locker room vet pick up the printed schedule of a season that had just begun.

"You know what sucks?" he asked, pointing at the home game calendar, "there's still *this* many games to go."

Like anyone else, they had other crap to do. The force of the universe was pulling at them to carry on with their adult lives.

But they just couldn't let it go.

Couldn't fathom losing it.

It had become central to their identity. Mine too. Being the guy with locker room access. The dude who spoke to NBA players. The buddy with a party bag of stories to share.[2]

Not even the richest fans in the city could acquire what we had.

One of them tried.

We'll call him Richie Rich.

Having successfully teamed up with his sister to sue their parents for half a billion bucks a piece, Richie was a twenty-something-year-old courtside staple. He had the four floor seats next to the visitors' bench nearest center court.

Ball boy rumor mill held that he'd asked the Bulls to make sure Derrick Rose said hi to him at games. True or not, Scottie Pippen – then employed as a Bulls "ambassador" – became his courtside counterpart. Benny the Bull became his good ol' buddy. A Luvabull cheerleader became his girlfriend.

Once, after a game, I watched Pippen walk him into the back lounge of the locker room by way of the laundry room doors. Richie, having purchased every other fragment of Bulls exposure that money could buy, hesitated. The sign above the door was written in plain English. He didn't belong. Pippen gestured for him to quit worrying and come on in. He did so, but nervously, and I never saw him in there again.

---

2. There's honestly not much of a story to be made of that time when you asked LeBron James where he got his forest green camouflage pants while he was buttoning his shirt at the bathroom sink mirror and you were actively using the urinal behind him, but tell it to six of your college pals while standing around a communal keg of Busch Light and the stage is yours. …By the time you get to the one about the game when you stuffed a thousand bucks cash in your sweatpants pocket at halftime after pulling it out of the public hallway ATM and then discreetly scurried back to the locker room to return Derrick Rose his debit cards without any of the bosses noticing, well, now you own the conversation.

I pranced through that same door moments later without batting an eyelash.

Money couldn't buy what we had.

So the vets, who no longer necessarily cared for it, held onto its keys. And the new guys, desperate to get more of it, never dared complain about the organizational dysfunction proliferated by those undying vets.

Things remained the way things had always been, in accordance with the way someone had once said they should be. Everybody knew how it was.

Nobody could tell you why.

And so it was that Flounder, a community college dropout, rose to prominence. As explained by Kevin D, Sharrod was technically top dog amongst our ranks, but Sharrod was a quiet, humble operator. He neglected the spoils of status that accompanied his throne.

So, Flounder made them his own.

Had Sharrod's number two been more like Sharrod, I might have never learned about the shadowy layers of a vet's locker room enterprise. But instead, his number two was Flounder, and Flounder relished being *that dude* in the eyes of whoever cared to see.

My eyes were wide open.

In his personal life, he was a suburban bachelor who lived with a couple of roommates; an older couple, who coupled as his parents. But outside the walls of his childhood bedroom residence, Flounder reigned supreme inside the underground walls of the United Center.

In the waning post-game moments of any given game night, when only Ligs, Joe Lee, a few security guards, and the ball boys remained, you'd find a common scene at the back corner of the laundry room.

With most of the fluorescent lights throughout the locker room hallways having been turned off, the ball boys would congregate in our boxers while changing out of our sweats. Everybody checking their cell phones for the texts from random friends who'd caught a glimpse of our heads in the background of their TV screen while watching the game. A ball boy or two inevitably stuffing a handful of leftover Bud Light cans into their backpack.

And there stood Flounder, openly thumbing through a wad of cash, counting his tip money like an outsized stripper after a fruitful shift. He'd flex just enough of his juice, and leak just enough of his insider scoops, to establish himself as our unholy leader.

I could never resist.

I wanted to know more about his recent evening spent at Chicago night clubs as the designated driver to Bulls players. More about that text Derrick Rose had recently sent him. More about the summer he spent as Kirk Heinrich's personal assistant. More about where he drove Luol Deng's car to run an errand before the game.

Flounder artfully positioned himself to have all subservient junior ball boys kissing his ring. And that ring was a cherry-flavored Ring Pop. One taste always had us coming back for more.

As for his game-to-game tasks, and a replicable picture of how he'd reached his exalted station in life, the details were kept obscure. You couldn't outwork him if you didn't know what he actually did.

"If any one of these players asks you for a favor, you come get me," Flounder once told me.

"*You* don't talk to the talent," he'd add, only half-jokingly, in another mentoring session.

While I had scant exposure to the *pre*-game locker room happenings in those early days, the *post*-game was an open arena on the Bulls side. It provided the dual opportunity of collecting my own occasional player interactions while also watching Flounder work his magic.

Ball Boy Commandment Number Two, while never clarified in the first place, was more practically interpreted by ball boys as "Control *the perception of* Your Pattern of Speech."

You wanted the trainers, Ligs, and anybody else of authority who might meander through the locker room while the players were getting dressed to be under the impression that you were dutifully speaking to no one unless called upon, while at the same time, managing to speak to any and all players you could find.

Player interaction was the currency everybody was after.

Oh, how I marveled at Flounder's graceful discretion in this category.

In my early experience, there was something distinctly nerve-wracking about talking to a player at his locker. Maybe it was the forbidden nature of the act. Or maybe it was the awkwardness of bothering a guy who was simply minding his own business as he got dressed after a hard day's work.

But, probably, it was just something I wanted so badly that when the opening arrived I couldn't figure out what to do with it. Precious moments of opportunity appeared and disappeared as I stared dumbfounded at an available player, frantically scouring my mind for a slick conversation starter.

Paralyzed.

Mute.

Barely audible at the times when I did work up the nerve to mumble a strike-out opener.

Damnit! Blew it again.

Why can't I be more like Flounder?!

These sacred player-interaction-enabling post-game locker room tasks revolved mainly around grabbing things off the floor and putting them where they belonged.

Used towels to the towel bin.

Ice water buckets to the wet room.

Shower sandals to wherever Ligs wanted the shower sandals to go.

"...and don't even think about packing them away without first diligently drying the water off each sandal with a towel you dumbass rookie!"

But the crowned jewel of post-game locker room floor loot was the collective contents of what's called a "loop."

A loop could be defined broadly as a collection of the *really* grimy stuff that soaked up a player's sweat while he played: underpants, undershirts, sweatbands, socks, etc.

To a pedestrian eye, the sweat-drenched underpants plopped down next to the naked man who'd just worn them might qualify as the *least* attractive item to pick up off the floor. But that's why you're the pedestrians, and we're the pros.

You don't understand.

What made this stinking, slimy, dripping collection of undergarments the prized treasure of our nightly post-game locker room prowl was not the items themselves, but rather the procedure that accompanied them.

Each item was to be organized into a band-like thing (the loop) that served to keep each player's crap organized for when Ligs did the laundry. Gathering a player's loop justified a ball boy's act of standing within conversational proximity to that player's locker while they got dressed.

An efficient laundromat employee might've gotten the loop together in fifteen or twenty seconds flat.

A proficient ball boy, on the other hand, could squeeze that slopping wet Fruit of the Loom for every drop of "serendipitous" conversational juice it held.

None performed this act better than Flounder.

Minutes dragged along as he clipped on the player's compression shorts, roped together the socks, finagled with the buckles and strings of the loop, before gradually finding the holster for the sweat bands and whatever else the player had worn that game to sponge up his sweat.

All conducted with ambitiously sloth-like speed.

Sultan of this post-game locker room turf, Flounder had his hands in everybody's loop. Whether the player wanted it or not, a hushed locker side chat awaited him after the game. There was no escaping. Flounder had him by the underpants.

Games turned into seasons.

Seasons stacked into years.

Player phone numbers entered Flounder's address book.

By the time I arrived, Flounder was synonymous with the Bulls locker room. A staple. How I envied his reign. But the clock always wins in the end.

Fast forward past my first few seasons.

Master though he may have been, as goes the predestined fate of any adult ball boy, even Flounder's carriage eventually turned into a pumpkin.

His, of course, erupted with fittingly dramatic flair.

As was the way things were done, the details of his termination were never outright shared with the rest of us, which laid fertile ground for our ball boy rumor mill. The clearest picture I gathered was that he'd been in a player's car, running an errand too close to game time, and then something came up back at the locker room. The trainers needed him, and he wasn't there to answer the call of duty.

The nature of this fatal violation was, of course, riddled in ambiguity.

Technically speaking, per Ball Boy Commandment Number Four, *Players Come First*, and Flounder was inevitably doing a favor for a player.

So, what's the crime?

Exactly.

But details be damned, at the end of the day his uncontrolled pattern of speech had simply rendered him too visible to fly under the radar anymore.

By the end, I'd overhear Bulls team captain Luol Deng making a case to my boss to bring him back. An unheard-of degree of player tampering into the happenings of the ball boy staff.

Even Luol's lobbying wasn't enough.

The bosses had grown tired of Flounder's impressive antics. The clock struck midnight on his legendarily stretched voyage through Ball Boy Land. His carriage turned to a pumpkin, and we never saw Flounder again.

Upon hearing the proverbial bell of Flounder's clock striking midnight, another junior ball boy, who'd become something of a protégé to Flounder, eulogized his legacy by speaking these words:

"Flounder will be fine. He's best friends with Derrick Rose."

It was the perfect statement, in that it accurately portrayed nothing of Flounder's relationship with Derrick

Rose, and yet everything of his perceived station amongst our ranks.

Flounder was Lord of the Ball Boys.

And if the Lord himself could be sacrificed for unspecified sins against our Ball Boy Commandments, well, then the bizarrely unprecedented situation that I would find myself in would surely be terminable.

But first, the Bulls had a seventh championship to win.

Chapter 3

Michael Jordan's Prophecy

Michael Jordan told a prophecy.

Trust me, I was right there.

It happened in April 2011 in front of twenty-two thousand Chicagoans.

"…You guys are in store for a lot of other championships," declared Jordan, standing center court with a microphone in his hand, addressing the sellout crowd that had gathered to honor the twentieth anniversary of the Bulls' first championship.

After the glory of the 90s came the drought of the early 2000s. But now we were in our third year since the fateful ping pong balls had bounced our way and the Bulls landed the number one draft pick the summer after my first season as a ball boy. That 2008 NBA Draft changed everything.

Enter Derrick Rose.

He was only a year older than me.

Upon the shoulders of that humble hometown kid, the Bulls were back.

Jordan looked over at the home side bench, which, on account of my position standing guard directly behind it, I considered to be His Airness looking directly at me too.

To my right sat Derrick Rose.

A few chairs to my left sat Joakim Noah.

"You look at this team tonight—"

Another roaring applause forced Jordan to pause and nod his head to acknowledge the crowd.

Derrick Rose was calmly attentive as we all watched MJ.

Joakim Noah was less calm.

"Don't be surprised," continued Jordan, "if you don't have six more coming."

Bonkers went the arena.

Goosebumps covered my arms.

Joakim Noah became a human golden retriever, gyrating in his chair and repeatedly smacking whoever's leg was next to his.

"His swag is *crazy* right now!" hollered Joakim, "Swag is *crazy!*"

From the lips of his most Holy, the prophecy was declared.

Don't be surprised when the Bulls win six more championships.

Eight weeks later, after the Bulls wrapped up the season with the first-place record in the league, another visitor arrived on May 5th: the Commissioner of the NBA.

Before the game, standing in the same spot where Jordan had declared his prophecy, Commissioner David Stern handed the Maurice Podoloff Trophy to twenty-two-year-old Derrick Rose.

"In a league of very valuable players," said Stern to Rose, "you are most valuable."

The crowd voraciously agreed.

Their hometown kid returned the love.

"This right here," replied Derrick, standing next to his mother and three brothers, "is for the city of Chicago more than anything."

Youngest MVP in NBA history.

Ten days later, LeBron James, Dwayne Wade, and the Miami Heat came to town for the 2011 Eastern Conference Finals.

Sunday, May 15, 2011. Game One.

It was the first time the Bulls had been to the Conference Finals since Jordan and Pippen beat Reggie Miller's Indiana Pacers in 1998.

In their three regular season matchups, the Bulls had swept the Heat.

Earlier in the day, a reporter asked Miami Heat head coach Eric Spoelstra a question:

"One theory is if you slow down Derrick Rose, you beat the Bulls," said the reporter. "Is it that simple?"

"Yea," replied coach Spoelstra with a smile. "Do you have an idea how to do that? He's MVP."

Warm-ups.

National Anthem.

Starting lineups.

Lights remained on as our stadium announcer provided the unenthusiastic, obligatory introduction of the Heat players. Fans booed. A guy up in the nosebleeds belted out "fuuuck you!" as the announcer wrapped up with the name "LeBron James."

Then somebody cut the lights.

The jumbotron displayed a video of a herd of animated Bulls storming through Chicago. Heavy drums played. When the herd of Bulls finally reached the parking lot of the

United Center, there was something in their way: the Miami Heat team bus. The herd of Bulls paused for a moment, thought about it, then charged ahead.

Smash.

Boom.

The Miami Heat team bus was demolished in a fiery explosion.

Then the drums stopped.

Piano keys hit.

Dun dun dun da-dun dun dun...

Everybody in Chicago knew the tune.

Screams amplified.

Then came that famous growl.

"Aaaaaaaaand now..." declared the stadium announcer, "the starting lineup, for *your* Chicagooo Bulls!!"

Carlos Boozer.

Luol Deng.

Joakim Noah.

Keith Bogans.

Steady cheers continued throughout. Then there was a momentary pause. The cheers turned into a roar. No, it was a thunder. Its volume matched the one they gave Michael Jordan at halftime three months prior.

Frooooom ChiCAgoooooo... !!!

Derrick Rose stood up from the chair in front of me, pounded two fists to his chest, kissed his fingers, waved at the fans who were now chanting "MVP!" and joined his team in the huddle.

Game time.

My revelation came with ten minutes and forty-two seconds remaining in the second quarter. That was the moment it all came into clarity.

The Bulls were down 22-25, but the moment had nothing to do with the scoreboard. It was about the energy that electrified the stadium when it happened. The goosebumps crawling up my arms once again.

I'd been working behind the Bulls bench during the game and got sent for an errand to the locker room. Returning to the court through the tunnel provided me an unobstructed line of sight to the court.

Something was happening.

I slowed my pace a bit to maintain my clear view.

It was a Bulls fast break, heading towards our basket.

A three-on-one against Dwayne Wade.

CJ Watson, unofficial captain of the Bulls' "Bench Mob," drove right. Wade beat him to the spot. CJ dished it back to a trailing Taj Gibson. Wade pivoted to get in position just as Taj, charging full steam ahead, caught the ball.

Ohhh shoot.

Here it comes!

Taj rose.

Wade rose.

Taj gripped the ball with two hands, arms stretched to the sky.

SLAM!

Had it occurred at a playground, the game would've stopped, and bystanders would've been dancing around the asphalt whooping and hollering crude remarks about Taj Gibson putting his something-or-other in Dwayne Wade's face.

But this wasn't a playground.

It was Game One of the NBA Eastern Conference Finals.

With the Bulls about to tie the game as Taj headed to the free throw line for the "and one," there was only one thought gripping my mind as I stood frozen in the walkway amidst the deafening sound of twenty-two thousand Chicagoans gone mad:

Holy shit.

This is really happening.

The Bulls are gonna win the Championship this year.

The momentum continued as the Bulls went on to beat the Heat by twenty-one points that night, claiming a 1-0 series lead.

"We're gonna sweep those motherfuckers!" hollered Bulls guard Keith Bogans after the game.

Then we lost the next four in a row.

While a 4-1 series loss may sound like a blowout, it wasn't.

"If you put all the scores together from that four-one series," recalled Joakim Noah years later, "the score was *fuckin' tied!*"

Painful.

But natural.

To get so close and lose was merely a required step along the destined path.

Just as the 90s Bulls had to overcome the Bad Boy Detroit Pistons before grasping the throne, so too would our 2010s Bulls need to lose to the Miami Heat before fulfilling Michael Jordan's prophecy.

Returning to the Conference Finals next season for a rematch with Miami was a foregone conclusion. Bulls Championship Number Seven was just around the corner. That much was predictable.

The left turn that awaited me senior year, was not.

Chapter 4

A White Whale's
Dirty D-Word

It was a cold morning in January 2012 as I walked down the block to Kasey Gandham's student apartment building.

Weeks prior, reigning MVP Derrick Rose bested Kobe Bryant with a game winning floater as the Bulls beat the Lakers in LA for the delayed Christmas Day opener of the lockout-shortened 2011-2012 NBA season.

Picking up right where we left off.

Having spent the offseason working for Kobe's world-famous trainer, I entered senior year feeling more assured than ever that my post-grad career would have something to do with the NBA.

Then, in November, alongside our friend Nick Currier, Kasey and I won first place in a business plan competition at Illinois State University.

Our proposed concept was to rent out digital textbooks by the day.

Only pay for what you use...

We're reversing the paradigm of heavy backpacks and light wallets...

And we're calling it "Packback"!

The central challenge of getting the business off the ground was the task of securing licensing rights to the content from textbook publishers. The good news was that most of the textbooks used in higher education were controlled by only a handful of publishers, namely the "Big Three": Pearson, McGraw-Hill, and Cengage. The bad news — aside from our utter lack of software coding skills to build a platform, funding to build a company, and any relevant career experience to effectively operate it — was that we didn't know anybody at those publishers.

Helping us out, one of Kasey's marketing professors had recently given him something useful.

Mike Boehm was the professor. He ran the sales education program at ISU, which positioned him to network with the sort of folks who are in the business of recruiting college students into sales careers. One of those folks happened to be a Vice President at Pearson.

His name was Brock Kirby.

Boehm handed Kirby's cell phone number to Kasey.

And that became our next task: cold call the VP at Pearson.

In preparation of the phone call, we did some last-minute background research. As it turned out, Mike Boehm's information was outdated. Brock Kirby was no longer a Vice President at Pearson. According to LinkedIn, he was now the *President* of McGraw-Hill Higher Education.

The man was a verified whale!

Better yet, his office was located a mere two hours from campus.

Smile and dial…

Given the nature of how I'd spent my winter break, my cold-calling axe was deemed sharpest on the team. The embarrassingly dangerous situation I'd gotten myself into that made it so was a secret I kept under wraps.

I'd gone to Milwaukee with some friends for New Years Eve.

Having netted something shy of a dollar-an-hour throughout my seventy-hours-a-week NBA offseason summer job, I was low on cash.

As went my logic, the bars were cheaper in Milwaukee than Chicago. Even cheaper than a Milwaukee bar was the bottle of lemon vodka at our apartment pregame party. And having spent much of my first semester ditching keg parties in exchange for long hours spent alone in the library buried in books that had nothing to do with my neglected homework assignments, my alcohol tolerance was running low.

Yea, blame it on the books.

Anyways, I took another swig of lemon vodka while awaiting a cab to the bars.

Then I woke up in the hospital with an IV sticking out of my arm.

Oops.

Apparently, as pieced together by my investigative questioning the next morning, I'd wandered off from my friends. At some point, my pal Max got a call from my cell phone, but it wasn't me talking on the other line.

A couple of Good Samaritan college girls had just found me passed out on the side of a building somewhere in downtown Milwaukee.

All told, the combined hospital and ambulance bills put me in the hole about a thousand bucks. So much for cost savings.

Hiking out of that hole, I spent my winter break flipping through grade school phone books, cold calling the parents of my younger siblings' friends, and attempting to sell them Cutco knives by slicing rope and leather in their kitchen.

How much you wanna bet I can cut that penny with this here pair of Cutco Super Shears?

It was a sizable drop from what I thought had become my new station in life, earned at a basketball kingdom called Attack Athletics.

Located on the west side of Chicago, Attack Athletics was a sixty-thousand-square-foot private training facility home to, among other closed-door events, the NBA Draft Combine. All sorts of NBA players trained at Attack during the offseason, and on Election Day 2008, even President Barack Obama stopped by for some pickup hoops while awaiting the election results.

I'd never heard of it until Bulls' athletic trainer Jeff Tanaka invited me to volunteer at the 2010 Draft Combine on behalf of the Bulls staff. It was there that I met, and subsequently emailed until he hired me, the owner of Attack Athletics. Perhaps the most famous strength and mindset trainer of all time, this was the man behind-the-scenes of Michael Jordan and Kobe Bryant:

Tim Grover.

It was a non-paid internship, and non-guaranteed that Tim would even keep you on staff all summer. The effective employment deal, as explained by Tim Grover in our opening staff huddle, was simple:

You do good work for us; we'll go to bat for you.

We've got people at every team in the league.

Deal.

With militant-like commitment, I *lived* at that gym all summer, as did some of my peers, who primarily came from team manager positions at premier Division I basketball programs. We'd be waiting outside in the morning for the boss's black SUV to pull up and unlock the high gate that surrounded the facility. It was the same gate that the neighborhood kids all tried climbing up when Kevin Durant rolled up for his Nike Camp one day. Our mentality became a point of pride: *beat Tim Grover to his own gym.*

In a matter of one summer, I'd made a lifetime of contacts across the league. Collected a ball boy career's worth of interactions with NBA players. Compiled over fifty pages of journaled notes detailing what I'd witnessed.

By the end of it all, I had earned my rank.

Rewarding my total surrender of any other priorities or relationships that summer, Tim Grover, who hadn't yet written his *New York Times* best seller, *Relentless*, and thus wasn't much for pleasantries and small talk, even gifted me a couple pairs of his hand-me-down shoes and engaged me in several career counseling conversations.[3] Then, on a light Sunday in which only two interns showed up for the optional day of work, he pulled me aside and told me to come see him in his office before I went home.

When I stepped inside the office, my direct manager, elite strength & nutrition trainer Matt Alarcon, was spelling out my last name as Tim wrote something down.

Then Grover held out his arm and handed me a five-hundred-dollar check.

---

3. When I considered pursuing a career as an NBA sports agent: "I know them all, and they're all dirty." Grover warned. When I contemplated the career stability of a coaching staff position: "In coaching, you go into it knowing that you're being hired to be fired. Even look at [Bulls Head Coach] Thibodeau. Just won Coach of the Year. If he has a couple of bad seasons he'll get fired too." *Yea right, Tim. That'll never happen to Thibs.*

Might as well have been ten million. Not since receiving the football "Scout Team Award" as a fourth-string defensive back my senior year of high school had I felt so acknowledged in the field of athletics. Before depositing it, I made a copy of the check and proudly framed it on my wall. The implication was worth more than the cash.

Tim Grover was Jordan and Kobe's guy.

Now I was one of Grover's guys. I'd have options.

My path to doing something real in the NBA was laid.

And yet there I was, months later, selling kitchen knives to church moms.

Kasey at my side, beer stains on the carpet, I plugged in the digits to cold call the President of McGraw-Hill, feeling that nervous feeling of standing on a high dive as I stared at the cell phone screen. All instincts of human comfort zone told me to stall, but my Cutco sales manager — a magnificently entertaining man named Danny Lewis — had taught me better than that. Hesitation kills a cold call.

Fuck it.

Smashed the dial button.

Pause. Ring.

As the speaker phone rang in my hand, Kasey was suddenly struck with a wave of last second revelations. A surplus of advice poured from his eager mouth into my nervous ear, forming a mixtape of flashy buzz verbiage that only the number one marketing student in the university could conjure.

Ring.

"...tell him we're *stream-lining* distribution..." something something something.

Ring.

"we're *revolutionizing*…" yadda yadda yadda.

Ring.

"…*guerilla* marketing tactics…" bla bla bla.

Ring.

"And make sure you say…"

Goddamnit, Kasey!

"Dude! Fine." I barked back at him, "Here, you say it then."

In a swell of nervous frustration, I handed the phone to Kasey.

Whatever.

Like the rest of them, this call was about to go to voicemail anyways. Scene will end, and Kasey and I will proceed into our latest arm-wrestling match of wantrepreneurial debates while loosely considering whether or not to attend class that day.

But the phone never went to voicemail.

"This is Brock."

Kasey and I flashed a look at each other.

Woah.

He actually picked up!

Kasey dove into the pitch.

Dazzling as it was, I don't recall a word of it. What my memory clung to was the treasure box of responses on the other end of the line.

Kasey opened by establishing our credibility as leaders amongst the ISU student body. He had been president of our co-ed business fraternity last year; I was the president this year.

"…Well, I definitely want to meet you," said Kirby, "because I'd like to *hire* you."

The logistics of how such a meeting may occur were briefly ideated.

"Maybe I'll send a limo to drive you guys up to Burr Ridge," Kirby continued, "we have *beautiful* offices in Burr Ridge."

Woah. I hadn't been in a limousine since high school prom, and who doesn't love a beautiful office? This all sounded amazing.

"...Or maybe I'll come to campus." He ideated.

Even better!

My goodness, Kasey was doing it. He was landing the President of McGraw-Hill. The call concluded with a follow-up action to loop Brock's assistant into an email thread. She'd help us find a time for a meeting in the spring.

Incredible.

I texted Nick:

Kasey just hooked the big fish.

By the end of our weeks-long email thread with Kirby's assistant, the event was booked. Promotional flyers soon plastered the walls of our college of business building. You couldn't stand in front of a urinal without being informed that Brock Kirby, President of McGraw-Hill, was scheduled to visit Illinois State University in March.

The event was an openly understood quid pro quo.

We'd leverage our student group leadership positions to open a campuswide audience to Kirby, complete with an evening auditorium speaking event, a classroom speaking tour, and a private dinner, per Kirby's request, with "eight of the brightest students we knew." In exchange, he agreed to hear us out on our proposal for McGraw-Hill to partner with Packback for rent-by-the-day eTextbook distribution.

At long last, the day arrived.

In preparation for his overnight stay, we collaborated with his assistant to make light of the logistics. A brand new Marriott hotel had recently opened right on the edge of ISU's campus. The perfect dwelling for our VIP to rest his C-Suite head at night.

But that's not where we sent Brock Kirby.

The Marriott guy informed us that they were fully booked. Something about a tire convention; the kind of thing that draws a hot crowd in central Illinois. So, we put Kirby up in one of the bargain truck-stop motels that populated Main Street in Bloomington-Normal. Our version of red carpet treatment was a far cry from the limousine he'd offered to send us.

Oh well.

Awaiting his arrival, we were seated in the basement atrium of the college of business. We sat there, eyes glued to the entrance doors atop the staircase, wearing our finest suits, ties, and church shoes. Our matching golden Alpha Kappa Psi Business Fraternity lapels carefully pinned to the left breast of each of our suit coats let people know that we meant business.

Then it happened.

The door opened.

Appearing at the top of the staircase was a large bald man, molded in the spitting image of B-list sitcom celebrity Drew Carey. Black suit. White shirt. *No* tie. Cool trendy glasses.

Our whale had arrived.

Having partnered with our rival business fraternity, DSP, to make it a more-or-less mandatory event for our collective student members, the auditorium was packed full.

Thus began our keynote speaker event.

Years later, over water cooler gossip swap at a conference, another McGraw-Hill executive would inform me that, rumor had it, when Brock Kirby was first being introduced to his McGraw-Hill employees at a sales kickoff, he attempted to convince the event hall staff to allow him to fly onto the stage from a hang gliding wire while motivational music blasted. Unfortunately, stringing up a wire and a harness strong enough to propel a two-hundred-something pound middle aged guy onto a stage for his business meeting was not within the core competencies, or safety protocols, of the event hall staff.

His supposed request was denied.

True or not, the point is that Kirby had a knack for the spotlight.

Upon taking center stage, he gripped our attention.

A former theatre kid, Kirby was a natural teller of stories. And he had a sales bag full of them. Growing up, he hadn't been a good student. Took a "sabbatical" from paying attention in class in the fourth grade. Scored a mere seventeen on his ACT. Wound up enrolled at a lower-tier State University, Western Illinois. Enlisted in the Army.

From these humble beginnings emerged the moment that changed everything: Brock Kirby's failed interview for a pharma sales job.

He was twenty-three years old, and he *really* wanted that job.

Too bad.

The hiring manager told Kirby that, although he wouldn't be giving him the job, he would tell him why he chose the other candidate. As went the story, while Kirby had prepared diligently for the *interview*, the other candidate went out and spoke to *customers*. She made it a no-brainer choice to hire her. That experience changed Brock Kirby's life, and the retelling of it parlayed right into the key moment of his keynote speech.

Kirby had a question for us, a riddle of sorts.

He reached into his pocket.

From his pocket he lifted a wallet. I can't tell you what it looked like, because my memory remains enchanted by what he pulled out of it: a crisp, one-hundred-dollar bill.

Lifting the bill into the air, he laid down the gauntlet.

There existed *one* word, he professed. A word that, beyond all other words, held the key to success. The degree to which we understood this word would define whether we'd live mere ordinary lives or propel ourselves into the rarified air of the "only one percent of people who reach their full potential."

We were salivating to know what it was.

Yet he'd only provide one hint: the first letter.

"I have a crisp, one-*hundred*-dollar bill" proclaimed Kirby, "for whoever can tell me what the *D-word* is?"

Instant murmur rippled through the crowd.

Kirby waved his Ben Franklin flag high and proud as a couple hundred business-casually-dressed college kids racked their brains for the answer to his riddle.

But I alone had the advantage.

In preparation for our meeting, I'd scoured Kirby's online presence. Read every word of his every blog post. I knew this man.

Several amateurs tried and failed to guess the answer.

Nope…

Wrong…

Close, but no...

I'd heard enough.

Step aside, classmates, it's time for the co-ed business fraternity President to end this.

Hand to the sky.

Kirby called upon me.

Without a trace of doubt in my voice, I delivered the big man his hundred-dollar word:

"Dirty."

A half moment of awkward silence.

Kirby gave a head-tilted look of confusion.

My friend, Ben, seated behind me, let out a hoot. That unlocked the floodgates.

An auditorium packed full of my AKPsi underlings and our DSP rivals erupted in laughter. Ben could hardly stay in his chair at the thought of it. I'd just implied that the single-most key to Brock Kirby's impressive success in conquering the mountains of higher education publishing was to be, of all things, *dirty*.

"No no no," I tried to recover, "what I meant was..."

Get your *hands dirty*.

He'd said something like that in a blog post somewhere. Swear to God. Didn't matter. Wrong answer. Next. When the laughter finally subsided, another kid guessed right.

"Differentiate."

Oh.

Yea that too.

Do that too, everybody. And don't be late for our chapter meeting next week.

Per Kirby, to be successful, you had to *differentiate* yourself. And here before us stood a man who'd done just that. Kirby had taken his seventeen ACT score, a brief stint in the Army, and a failed pharma sales job interview, mixed 'em up in a cereal bowl, and D-worded the crap out of himself.

D-worded himself straight to the top.[4]

And now I was coming for him.

Forget Mr. & Mrs. Condron and the three-hundred-dollar set of kitchen knives I'd sold them over winter break. *This* guy. He was it. This guy was Major League. Brock Kirby would be my great white whale. I just knew it.

Wrapping up the evening, a small group of us personally escorted Kirby back across campus to the bookstore parking lot where he'd parked his little white rental sedan. It was a metered spot. Stuffed under his windshield wipers was a pair of orange envelopes.

Everybody handed Kirby their student business cards.

Kirby handed me both of his orange envelopes.

"Here," he said, gifting me the parking tickets, "can you take care of these for me?"

Absolutely I would.

The show continued the next day with our tour of classrooms.

It being talent recruitment season, two HR reps had been assigned to join Kirby on his campus trip. Upon arrival, they did what campus recruiters do: set up a folding table, adorned it with a McGraw-Hill-branded tablecloth, and stood behind it in an unspoken plea for any and all students to grab a pamphlet off the table.

An *un*differentiated approach if ever there was one.

These were not Kirby's people.

---

4. Commander of an army of campus hallway loiterers schlepping around next edition textbook samplers to academic hermits hiding contently in their closet-sized paper-jammed offices.

"Look at them," he told us, with a nod of disapproving amusement. "Look. You see that? They just stand there."

Disgusting.

Kirby was no bystander. He was a hunter. And with that subtle shun of his HR team, we marched their boss straight into our classroom.

Kasey couldn't make it until later in the day, so it was Nick, Kirby, and me. Scarcely had I ever felt so important, standing suit-clad next to Nick, introducing a big dog executive to a collection of our peers who'd barely changed out of their pajamas in time for morning class.

I now present to you, the guy in charge of the people who sell the expensive textbooks that our professors make us buy.

We were legends in the making.

Kirby dove right in.

The fourth-grade sabbatical from paying attention in class. The seventeen ACT score. The Army stuff. The girl who beat him in the pharma sales interview. It was the same song and dance as the night before, albeit with slightly lower stakes.

"I've got a crisp *fifty*-dollar bill in my wallet" proclaimed Kirby, "for whoever can tell me what the *D-word* is…"

The first class we visited was taught by Professor Joe Solberg, a Notre Dame Law School grad who'd opted out of practicing law for a more leisurely lifestyle teaching Business Ethics in central Illinois.

Kirby was, of course, the opposite of leisurely.

A favorite professor amongst students, known for his quick wit, a smirk never left Solberg's face as Kirby hijacked his classroom. For the remainder of the semester, whenever asking me how the project was coming along, Professor Solberg referred to Kirby by a new nickname:

How's Mister-in-Your-Face doing? Ha ha ha!

But he knew what we were pursuing, so our professor generously went along with the act. Ashley won the prize, Solberg bit his tongue, and we moved on to the next classroom.

Kirby stepped boldly inside.

Same play. Different result.

These students were disinterested. They lacked the muster of an audience deserving of Brock Kirby. He cut the talk short. Nick and I followed him out into the hallway like a pair of Secret Service agents.

Ouch, I thought.

He must be embarrassed.

Wrong.

Kirby doesn't get embarrassed. He teaches lessons.

"You see what I did there?" he asked us, "Cut it short. They were losers."

Kirby's time was money, and the money goes to the winners.

When the classroom talks adjourned, it was our turn to dazzle.

Kasey joined us in the College of Business board room that the Dean let us borrow for this important occasion. The boardroom was where we'd unveil our prized asset. Purchased with the "in kind services" awarded by a local printing shop to the winners of the ISU business plan competition, and artfully designed by our friend Jessica Tenuta, the asset was an oversized pamphlet-sorta-thing that, across seven thick pages, illustrated how daily eTextbook rentals would work.

The pamphlet was so glossy that the pages stuck together and made a distinct squeaking noise when you turned them. Most dazzling of all was page two, home to the six steps of the Packback user experience:

Enter → *Login* → *Purchase* → *Need* → *Read* → *Succeed*

Brock Kirby, prepare to have your mind blown.

The journey up to the boardroom provided our latest window for small talk with Kirby. A chance to get to know one another at a personal level.

He had a lot to tell us.

Kirby's expertise knew no bounds and begged no questions of doubt. In the hallway to the board room, he took a moment to explain that "if I knew in college what I know now," meaning, if he possessed his modern day differentiated sales acumen, then he would have "crushed it" in the dating game.[5]

By the time we were seated at the boardroom table, Kirby was further explaining that those same selling abilities would now make him an excellent Division I college football coach. Even though he'd never played football before.

"I guarantee it," he declared, on the basis that coaching Division I college football was all about recruitment, and recruitment was all about sales.

He was the modern day Renaissance Man. Down to earth and up in the stars all at the same time. Kirby liked Kanye West. *Loved* Taylor Swift. Was a huge fan of Ultimate Fighting, "for the *strategy* of it." He watched talent shows on his couch at night, just like anybody else, "but the difference is, I'm also writing a blog post at the same time."

---

5. I cannot overemphasize how closely in appearance he resembled B-List sit-com celebrity Drew Carey as we nodded along in agreement to the guaranteed romantic success he would have won with the ladies if only his D-word was a little bigger back in college.

I asked him about books. He didn't have much time for books, but he read *tons* of articles, TechCrunch and stuff. His favorite TV show, which he told us we *have* to watch, was called Shark Tank.

I'd never heard of it.

Naturally, my ball boy stories entered the dialogue. Kirby enjoyed that. The New York headquarters of McGraw-Hill was located in the corporate building attached to Madison Square Garden, home of the Knicks.

"You and me and are gonna go to a game at the Garden one day," he promised, "and I'm *serious* about that."

Count me in!

He was a marketing expert, and naturally knew a thing or two about branding. On that topic, we had a problem.

"The name sucks," he proclaimed, "Back-pack-pa…"

He paused to untangle his twisted tongue.

"…Paaack. …*back?* What is that? It's gotta be something catchy, like twentyfourhourtextbooks.com or something."

We didn't linger on the topic for too long. There was plenty more to cover. More advice to soak in. Kirby had more places to go in life. He warned us not to accept too much from corporate.

"…because then they own you." He explained.

At that, when I asked him what he'd do next, now that he was at the top, he talked about being willing to let it go. He had plans to write a book about leadership one day. I planned to be the first to read it.

Eventually, we got to the meat of our Packback pitch.

One glossy, squeaking page turn at a time, we walked him through our pamphlet. Never had such a simple concept been portrayed with such prolongated beauty, grace, and big vocabulary buzz words:

Packback offers a revolutionary 24-hour digital textbook rental service...

Packback's 24-hour rental model is conducive to the redefinition of the relationship between publishers and consumers...

By effectively eliminating consumer cognitive dissonance in textbook expenditures through an e-book medium...

By the end of it, I couldn't tell you if Kirby had listened to anything I said, but I was certain that he liked the way I said it. During the elevator ride back down to the atrium, he and I found ourselves together at last, in private. Something of a sales guy romance was forming.

"You're ready," he told me, "I'd hire you *today*. The other guys? Not quite there yet."

Nick was pursuing an advanced five-year Accounting MBA program and had no plans of venturing into textbook sales. Kasey was a soon-to-be Bone Scholar, the University's single highest academic honor, contemplating a variety of promising career opportunities. Perhaps Kirby recognized that I was his only viable lead of the bunch. Nonetheless, his praise pumped adrenaline through my veins.

"...You *get it*." he concluded.

From one President to the next.

The adrenaline of the day flashed into evening and before long it was time for dinner. Per his instructions, we'd gathered eight of the best & brightest students that we knew, worthy of an audience with Brock Kirby.

He didn't bother to invite his HR reps.

As Kasey, Nick, and I walked out of the College of Business with Kirby, the question arose of who would ride to the restaurant with him? I volunteered for the spot. Let the romance continue.

The two of us got into his little white rental sedan together.

"You like cars?" he asked me, as he pulled out of the parking garage.

"Not really" I replied, as I stepped onto my collegiate idealist soapbox, explaining something about cars being an unwise badge of status, etc. etc.

Kirby nodded along to my sermon and then carried on unaffected.

"I'm thinking about a Maserati," he said, "or maybe a Jeep."

The implication was that he made money. *Big* money. If I followed him, maybe I would too. The car ride continued.

Kirby took a phone call from one of his sales leaders.

"Gus!" he hollered, "What are you even *doin'?!*"

They talked goals. *Big* goals.

"You're gonna have to have a bonus of like three hundred 'K' this year!" Kirby exclaimed to Gus.

After his phone call, our conversation continued.

Kirby hadn't realized that I was the President of the co-ed business fraternity that he'd spoken in front of the night before.

"You're the *President?!*" he clarified, "Of that whole group? Good for you man!"

My chest got a little bigger. The praise carried on. And then, as if struck by divine revelation, Kirby saw my future flash before his eyes.

"You're the type of guy who'll own a chain of Taco Bells one day because you understand scaling!" he proclaimed.

Of the business model we were actually pitching him, Kirby was doubtful. And yet, of the ability of the Irish kid sitting in his passenger seat to one day operate a chain of Mexican fast-food restaurants, he was unflinchingly confident.

At dinner, Kirby owned the table.

He ordered *two* beers. He laughed with us. He interviewed us. He preached to us. At one point, he stood up from his chair. There was music playing in the background; it spoke to him. His shoulders started moving rhythmically. Years later, this moment would have a lasting impact on some of the dinner attendees.

Hey, remember when that McGraw-Hill guy started dancing at dinner? So weird.

I saw nothing weird about it.

That's just what big ballers do at business dinners.

The evening didn't result in a closed deal, but we won the next best thing: the promise of a follow-up meeting with other key executives at McGraw-Hill's suburban office.

The beautiful one.

After dinner, he stepped back into his little white rental sedan, and Brock Kirby headed home. I went home too, adrenaline still pumping, and cranked out a multi-page blog post:

Title: *McGraw-Hill's Maverick*

These past two days, the Illinois State campus was graced with the presence of Brock Kirby, president of McGraw-Hill Higher Education. He made the grand voyage down to Normal, IL with plans to meet students as well as learn about a fresh new start up business, Packback (which promises to break the mold of stagnant textbook purchasing models while providing a phenomenal service mutually beneficial to both publishers and students). In addition to giving his much-valued insight on an already "lights out" business proposal, Brock's visit impacted campus immensely...

Chapter 5

The Day the Music Died

"So," asked Bulls forward Carlos Boozer, "what do you do when you're not working here?"

He and I were the only two people in the back players' lounge as I folded my bin of towels and he ate his pre-game meal.

Screw it, nobody's watching, just tell him.

"...I'm also working on starting a business," I admitted, while placing a newly folded towel on the stack before grabbing another one from the bin.

"Oh yea?!" Boozer replied. "What kind?"

I explained the idea.

Helping students save money on expensive textbooks...

Only pay for what you use...

All the punchlines.

"Oh, that's a great idea, bro!" he replied, "I remember back at Duke..."

Remarkable.

Even Carlos Boozer had a bone to pick with overpriced textbooks.

Packback was becoming real.

And so was Michael Jordan's prophecy.

Five weeks after Brock Kirby departed Bloomington-Normal, the Philadelphia 76ers arrived in Chicago. The 2012 NBA Playoffs were upon us.

Two days before the playoffs began, on April 26, 2012, Benny the Bull handed a microphone to fan-favorite Brian Scalabrine at center court to address the United Center fans before the final regular season game of the year.

The Bulls had, for the second season in a row, secured first place.

"Chicago fans, it's been a long year," said Scalabrine. "You guys came out and supported us every night. For that, we are thankful. But the playoffs are about to begin, and we're going to need you. Every possession. Every game. Every series. We're gonna need your energy. We're gonna need your energy to get us through that fight. To fight every night. To win…"

Scalabrine pointed up to the far end of the stadium ceiling where the Jordan era championship banners hung.

"…banner number seven right there."

The crowd went wild.

Game One was a Saturday noon tipoff. When security guard Karen cracked open the door to Gate Three and a Half early that morning, I was the lone ball boy standing outside waiting for her, wearing a formal button-up shirt and tie because, well, it was playoff time dammit.

Intensity across the United Center was heightened for the playoffs.

A golden lab dog sniffed me for bombs while I filled the Gatorade jug in the wet room. Police force German Shepherds roamed the hallways.

The same intensity had its grip on the warmup shooting drills.

I took the Bulls side to ensure that premium rebounding flow was provided.

Per usual, assistant coach Adrian Griffin was warming up rookie Jimmy Butler. What was unusual was Coach Griffin's tenacity. He was typically on the calmer side of the coaching sphere. Not today. Something irked him.

He was all over Jimmy.

"Game shots!" coach Griff commanded, "Take *game* shots!"

Jimmy Butler wasn't one to complain or slack off, but his back hurt.

Their discourse picked up. Griff hollered at Jimmy. Jimmy talked back. I snagged a rebound and dished it to Coach Griff who passed it to Jimmy for the next shot. Both men kept barking at each other as the cycle continued. It reached a peak intensity and then... nothing.

Jimmy Butler's warmup drills were done.

They shook hands on good terms. No hard feelings.

It was simply playoff time.

A while later I looked up and saw Benny the Bull suspended by a wire in midair, flailing his arms in a practice dance as the song "Enter Sandman" by Metallica bellowed out of the stadium speakers.

"I need to get this," said assistant Coach Ed Pinckney to Carlos Boozer, "listen to this in the car ride here next game."

"Yes, you do!" confirmed Boozer.

The conversation evolved into a question about who would be singing the national anthem before the game. Coach Ed had a favorite: a retired Blackhawks hockey player named Jim Cornelison.

Well known for his deep, commanding voice, when Jim Cornelison sang the national anthem the United Center crowd turned up their volume with him.

Backup point guard Mike James, whose voice resembled that of Mike Tyson, entered the conversation.

"They gotta let me sing the national anthem," said Mike James.

"No, you gotta hear my man sing, just wait," explained Coach Ed, "I think they're saving him for Miami."

All roads led to an Eastern Conference Finals rematch against the Heat. Everybody knew it. And the Bulls were ready for it.

Earlier in the regular season, after a home win against Miami, I was snatching shower towels off the floor of the Bulls locker room during post-game pre-media time, soaking in the team dialogue.

"That's too easy," said Rip Hamilton, in reference to the Bulls's approach to stretching Miami's defense, "too easy."

All roads lead to Miami.

Let's get this first round over with.

When pre-game rebounding wrapped, my fellow ball boys and I darted over to the media room for a quick pre-game lunch. The place was packed.

A who's who of sports media personnel.

Hey there's Sheryll Miller!

Her brother, Reggie, and his game analyst colleagues were in the visitors' hockey locker room that doubled as the TNT room.

I wolfed down my lunch, ran back to the Bulls laundry room to grab my Adidas-mandated flat brim hat, and hit the court in time to claim my in-game turf:

Bulls-side behind the bench.

I took the chair behind assistant coaches Mike Wilhelm and Rick Brunson.

By the time we reached the final name of the starting lineups, there wasn't a calm voice in the stadium.

Frooommmmm ChiCAgooo…!!!

Game time.

The series had an underlying narrative, revolving around Derrick Rose and the Sixers' Evan Turner, who was also a Chicago kid. As went the story:

While in high school, Rose and Turner were the number one and number two ranked players in the state, Rose being number one. When their respective teams, Simeon and St. Joe's, met in a notable tournament, words were exchanged. Rose emerged victorious.

After the game, Evan Turner spoke to a reporter.

Then, that reporter went and spoke to Derrick Rose's coach.

Rose's coach, upon hearing what Turner had said, asked the reporter to walk with him down a hallway. They arrived at a curtain. When the coach pulled it back, there sat Derrick Rose with his older brother, Reggie.

"Tell him the quote," said the coach to the reporter.

"He didn't do anything when I was guarding him," Turner had told the reporter. "He knows I was better today."

At that, the ordinarily quiet, young Derrick Rose responded:

"We both know who's better. He's just looking for some attention," said Derrick. "We'll see who goes on to do more at the next level."

Fast forward to the 2012 NBA Playoffs, his Sixers being the heavy underdog in the matchup, and Turner rekindled the old flame. Asked by a reporter what he thought it meant to face the Bulls instead of the Heat in the first round, Turner replied:

"It means we're dodging the tougher team. That's what I think."

Thus, the Chicago Sun Times had their cover story.

Two hometown faces stamped with two headline words: *Bad Blood*

I'd had a few interactions with Evan Turner. First, when he was an incoming rookie at the 2010 NBA Draft Combine, and then later while I was working in the Sixers' locker room during a regular season game. I found him to be an especially nice guy. Polite. Personable. Humorous.

Quite honestly, he was a true man of the ball boys, and I really liked Evan Turner.

Who cares. It's playoff time.

When Turner checked into the game off the bench late in the first quarter, twenty-two-thousand fellow Chicagoans boo'd their unloved *other* hometown kid.

The choir of boos continued every time Turner touched the ball.

Sorry kid, this is exclusively Derrick Rose's town now.

As the game progressed, two events occurred that struck me as bad news for the Philadelphia 76ers.

The first one involved Evan Turner.

After fouling Joakim Noah under the basket in the third quarter, Turner bumped twice into Carlos Boozer and lightly pushed him in the back. Tempers rose. Rip Hamilton stepped in to exchange words with Turner. Sixers' big man

Elton Brand got involved. The referees intervened, but not before the little dust up caught the attention of Derrick Rose.

Atypical of Rose, he started clapping in Turner's direction, earning himself a rare technical foul.

Uh oh.

Now you got him fired up.

The second event occurred in the fourth quarter.

Ordinarily a resident of the midrange, Rose ventured out to the three-point line. When he drained one, the crowd cheered.

Then he hit another.

Then *another.*

When Carlos Boozer and Rip Hamilton instinctively leapt off the bench, the TNT cameras caught their celebratory reaction, along with my smirking face behind them. With 6:02 remaining in the fourth quarter, the latest D-Rose three-pointer had put the Bulls up by twenty. But it wasn't the scoreboard that struck me as bad news for the Sixers, it was Derrick's facial expression:

A full grinned smiled.

Uh oh.

Now he's having fun again.

As we approached the final minute of the fourth quarter, the Bulls still held a commanding lead, but the momentum was shifting. The Sixers had chipped the margin down to twelve with a minute twenty-seven seconds remaining.

To quell the momentum shift, Coach Thibs left the starters in the game.

The stats on the Jumbo-Tron displayed Derrick Rose at 23 points, 9 rebounds and 9 assists, thus planting a fun twofold buzz in the crowd:

D-Rose might snag a playoff triple-double, and everybody might get a free McDonalds Big Mac if the Bulls scored above a hundred points.

My attention shifted to the post-game ball boy duties.

Game One's in the bag.

Time to get the towels in the laundry bin.

Derrick Rose dribbled the ball up the court.

Fans watching on national television listened to the voice of Reggie Miller:

"...exactly what he's supposed to do. Because the Bulls are trying to send a message, and a knockout punch, that 'look, we're looking to sweep you guys...'"

Derrick took a high pick from Joakim Noah and dribbled to the top of the three-point line. Slight hesitation, then he turned on the jets to attack the hoop.

Referencing Evan Turner, Reggie Miller kept talking.

"You wanted us..."

Derrick drove baseline right. Jump stopped.

"You were crying out that...

Landing from the jump stop, Derrick bounced back up in the air as if to take a floater shot, but instead dished the ball to Carlos Boozer on his right.

"You bypassed the harder team, the Miami Heat..."

Derrick landed.

He held his knee.

Hobbled a few steps as his back arched forward.

"Uh oh! Uh oh!" hollered Marv Albert, cutting off Reggie Miller. "Rose came down bad on his left foot! You see him?! Holding onto his knee... Holding onto his knee... And down!"

Somebody on the Bulls missed a shot.

Somebody on the Sixers got a rebound.

Who cares.

When five Sixers players ran down to our side of the court to play offense, only four Bulls players returned on defense.

Derrick Rose remained on the other side of the court.

He was on his back. Then his side. Eyes wincing. When a visitor's side ball boy observed Sixers coach Doug Collins ask Derrick if he was alright, he didn't respond.

He's still holding onto his knee.

Foul. Whistle.

Joakim Noah sprinted back to the other side of the court to check on Derrick.

Head Trainer Fred Tedeschi was fast behind, followed by Carlos Boozer.

Soon to follow was team Doctor Brian Cole, Rose's security guard, Coach Thibs, and our boss Jeff Tanaka.

As Derrick lay wincing on the ground, the crowd emerged spontaneously into a chant that bellowed and grew across the United Center.

M-V-P! ...M-V-P! ...M-V-P! ...M-V-P!

The chants graduated to applause as Fred and Jeff lifted Derrick to their shoulders for an assisted walk off the court.

Bulls won 103 to 91.

Everybody got a Big Mac.

Nobody knew whether or not to celebrate it.

With the loudspeaker amplifying his voice across the stadium for the post-game interview, Joakim Noah asked everybody to say a prayer for Derrick.

Ordinary post-game ball boy routine ensued.

As Thibodeau convened the closed-door team meeting in the locker room, I wheeled the Bulls-side Gatorade cart into the wet room right outside of the door. When I turned around to face the trainer's tables, there he was.

Derrick Rose.

He was lying face-up on the trainer's table nearest the wet room with his leg propped up by some device. His older brother, Reggie, stood by his side along with Fred, Jeff, and Dr. Brian Cole.

Standing fifteen or so feet away from his table, while a couple of fellow ball boys and I lingered silently at the wet room door awaiting the end of Coach Thibodeau's team meeting, I did what came naturally: I stared blankly.

Derrick Rose turned his head, and, for a split second, we made accidental eye contact.

He had tears in his.

I looked away, feeling guilty. There was the cornerstone of the Bulls' long-awaited return to glory, the high-flying hometown kid, grounded on his back with a leg propped up, unable to join the post-game meeting with his teammates.

He didn't deserve to be stared at by the ball boys.

Before long, the entire Bulls front office brass would make their way to Derrick's table to check on him. Gar Foreman. John Paxson. Randy Brown. Organization staff aside, that red trainers' table on which he laid had become the unseen eye of a media storm brewing outside of the guarded doors of the Chicago Bulls locker room.

When the team meeting ended, the internal locker room door opened to the ball boys.

The media remained locked out.

It wasn't the usual pre-media fun time that we'd become accustomed to with this team. Nobody was laughing.

One by one, the players went to see Derrick.

For a fleeting moment there remained a glimmer of optimism in the fog.

CJ Watson came back to his locker after talking to Derrick.

"What'd he say?" asked Ronnie Brewer, "is it nothing?"

Here's hoping.

At one point, between carrying ice buckets back to the wet room, I even observed Assistant General Manager Randy Brown land a joke that got Derrick to crack a smile. But the prevailing mood in the locker room was somber.

More like the lobby of a funeral home than the afterparty of a playoff victory.

Ronnie Brewer returned to his locker after his turn visiting Derrick.

"He said the leg came *out*, and he had to pop it back in," recalled Ronnie. "What does that mean? You can't dislocate your *leg*. Maybe his knee just popped out for a second?"

I stood at the center of the Bulls logo that covered the locker room floor, unsure where to move. I wasn't hunting for underwear-loop locker-side player dialogue. Nobody wanted to chat with a ball boy in that moment.

I looked over at Carlos Boozer.

He was sitting with his head down, hands together in prayer.

A common theme.

Sometime later I overheard Mike James rhetorically ask Luol Deng, "What can ya do?"

"Pray," responded Luol.

Minutes evaporated in the eerie stillness of the sullen locker room.

Then, suddenly, there was a holler somewhere outside, in the direction of the coaches' room. Confrontation had occurred in there before.

"Over!" was all that could initially be heard. "Move over!" commanded a baritone voice just beyond the locker room front door. *"MOVE! ...OVER!"*

The abrupt tenacity caught the attention of Carlos Boozer.

"What's that?" Boozer asked, as if ready to intervene, "What was that?!"

"Security," someone assured him, "it's just security."

"Oh," replied Boozer, "I like that. I like aggression."

That a security guard was brought to such volume meant only one thing: the surrounding media storm was gaining steam and losing patience.

They wanted in.

A few minutes later, Bulls de facto media gatekeeper, Shaun Hickombottom, poked his head in and informed the players, apologetically:

"I gotta let them in guys."

"Give me a minute." said Boozer.

"Ok," said Shaun, then he pointed at Rip Hamilton, "you don't have to talk."

I wasn't privy to the reasoning behind which players had to talk to the media after the game or not, but it didn't take an insider's scoop to understand who they were most keen on finding.

Didn't matter.

He wasn't available.

After the Boozer-requested extended minute, the front door was finally opened. In poured an avalanche of reporters and camera crews.

E-Buck, the Bulls security guard who focused specifically on Derrick Rose, rushed in and muscled his way through the mob of media personnel to the empty corner locker. He grabbed Derrick's shoes, then maneuvered his way back out through the door next to Jordan's still-vacant former locker which led to the trainer's room.

The media couldn't enter that door.

But I could.

When I walked through it and looked up, the medical staff were putting Derrick's shoes on for him. He was wearing a Chicago Bulls sweatsuit, denied the simple pleasure of a post-game shower after sweating through thirty-seven minutes of gameplay, second only to Luol Deng's thirty-nine.

Someone handed him a pair of crutches.

After hobbling off the trainer's table, his head down, body sore, spirit shattered, Derrick Rose made his way down the back hallway.

His security guard went in front of him and, as if preparing soldiers for battle, directed the small fleet of other security guards, who were waiting in the back hallway, on which corners to cover.

Then the twenty-three-year-old reigning MVP crutched himself out the back laundry room door.

Derrick Rose's departure was unceremonious enough that not everybody even noticed. Carlos Boozer, still getting dressed after a round of media questions, looked over at me when I returned to the locker room.

"He left already?" asked Boozer.

"Yea," I confirmed.

Boozer hung around the locker room for a little while longer then departed out the back. I was in the players' lounge when he passed.

"Man," said Boozer, extending farewell fist bumps to another ball boy and me, "I just feel so bad for that mo' fucker."

"Yea," I replied, with a head shake.

"He just can't catch a break," added Boozer.

"I know," I concurred.

With that, Boozer embarked out the same back laundry room hallway path as Derrick had. Before he left, he glanced at the big screen TV in the lounge. The New York Knicks were playing the Miami Heat.

"I hope New York busts ya'll ass," said Boozer to the television.

Soon thereafter, wearing a blue suit and tie, Luol Deng gathered a plate of food from the buffet tray in the lounge while the ball boys congregated. We were waiting for the jerseys to finish their laundry cycle so we could hang them up to dry in the equipment closet.

A colleague of mine apparently couldn't read the room.

"We're just waiting for these *players* before we can get our food," joked the ball boy.

"Come on guys," Luol replied, his smiling tolerance for the poorly timed joke providing a testament to his good character.

"It's all good as long as we got that 'W'" said Joe Lee, in a well-meaning but tired refrain he'd been repeating throughout the locker room since the game ended.

Luol nodded in pretend agreement, but his mind was elsewhere.

Rip Hamilton entered the room as Luol finished scooping the food onto his plate.

"Man," said Luol, "I never felt so bad after a win."

"I know, man," replied Rip, "I'm still fucked up."

With the laundry cycle about to finish, our boss, Jeff Tanaka, stood in the back laundry room with us. Breaking the awkward silence, that same situationally tone-deaf ball boy asked Jeff:

"So, what's your inside information?"

"There isn't any," replied the man who'd just carried Derrick Rose off the court, "I know how Twitter works too."

Having hung up the jerseys to dry, all post-game duties were complete. It appeared that everyone but the ball boys had left. The coast looked clear. I decided to grab some food.

There were only a few noodles and string beans left anyways.

As I scooped what little remained of the buffet cart onto my plate, in walked coach Tom Thibodeau.

"Is there any even left?" he asked, to nobody in particular.

Shit!

Coach Thibs hasn't eaten yet.

I immediately stopped filling my plate and got out of his way. Coach looked defeated. My mind flashed to the career advice conversation I'd had with Tim Grover eight months earlier:

In coaching, you go into it knowing that you're being hired to be fired. Even look at Thibodeau. Just won Coach of the Year. If he has a couple of bad seasons, he'll get fired too.

Media headlines and debate-show questionnaires were already swarming to the sizzling hot topic of whether Derrick Rose should have been in the game with less than two minutes remaining and the Bulls up by twelve points.

Tragedy craves a scapegoat.

Coach Thibs was suddenly its prime candidate.

And now there he sat, alone on an empty couch in the back lounge of an empty locker room. Not a single piece of protein on his post-game meal plate. Hunched over, picking at what was, thanks in part to me, a minimal selection of string beans and noodles, watching in silence as the Knicks played the Heat.

For some reason I felt like I needed to say goodbye to him.

I walked back into the room, acting like I was looking for a fork.

"Take care, coach," I said.

"Alright," replied the reigning NBA Coach of the Year to the ball boy who stole his noodles.

The bright afternoon spring sunshine beaming upon the United Center parking lot felt unnatural, juxtaposed against the somber, windowless locker room we'd just departed.

The bleak of midnight would have been more appropriate.

They say denial is the first stage of grief.

"Damn," a fellow ball boy remarked, "he may be out through Boston."

Yea.

Out through Boston.

The presumed second round of those playoffs.

But we could get through Boston. Derrick Rose would be back for Miami in the Eastern Conference Finals rematch. It was all a part of the plot to Michael Jordan's prophecy.

Don't be surprised if you don't have six more championships coming with this team.

I got in the car and headed south for my two-hour drive back to Normal, Illinois. With assorted hip-hop music on loud per usual, the city surroundings soon laid way to cornfields.

Buzz.

It was a text message from my dad.

Torn ACL.

Out for the season.

Face flush. Body chills. I turned off the music and rode back to school in dead silence. There was nothing to say. And not a song worth singing.

What can ya do?

Pray.

Chapter 6

The Big Bad Thing

Fall 2017. Three years since my retirement as a ball boy.

By the time the Big Bad Thing happened, I'd been awaiting the phone call for weeks. Pursuing the subject of it for over a year. At that point, Packback had already lived, died, been reborn again as something else, squared off in our would-be final battle with Goliath, and slayed the fucker.

It was time to tie the bow with a real venture capital term sheet. Validate our six years of punching at the entrepreneurial bag. Sail onwards toward success.

But success is a sly old wrinkly bastard.

"...that brings us to 2.9 million," said Troy Williams, Partner at New York-based venture capital firm University Ventures, as he explained the pre-money valuation of the term sheet he was preparing to send me.

My stomach turned to knots.

Some time ago he'd forecasted to me that his term sheet would be modest, likely a "flat round" on our latest angel investment valuation, something in the ballpark of $11 million pre-money valuation.

But this was no flat round.

The words echoed in my head as he carried on explaining the logic, which was indeed rich with reason albeit bankrupt of warmth.

$2.9 million pre-money valuation, on a cap table that already entailed $5 million dollars of capital raised across a hundred or so individual investors, was a very bad thing.

In startup circles of the day, everybody watched an HBO comedy show called *Silicon Valley*. In one of the episodes, a character named Monica went behind the back of her VC boss to provide honest valuation advice to a startup founder named Richard:

"…if you have a down round, you're *fucked*," explained Monica, "it is the kiss of death for a young CEO."

I didn't know it then, but the deal described by Troy didn't constitute a mere down round. It was worse. Something called a *re-capitalization*.

Troy wrapped up.

"So, yea. I just wanted to give you a call before doing the work to prepare the term sheet," he said, "to see if that would be a 'fuck you' hang-up."

Believe you me, by the fall of 2017, I'd been down the library halls. I'd read the literature. Books such as *Venture Deals* by Brad Feld, deemed mandatory reading for Tech Stars founders, confidently outlined the playbook on how to line up all your VC term sheets simultaneously to play them off each other.

That's how, as an entrepreneur, you were supposed to gain leverage.

Sounds simple enough while sitting in the library.

But out on the field, there exists not a playbook for how to optimally respond when the lone venture capitalist standing up amidst your red sea of VC rejections politely asks you if your response to his proposed terms — your *only* available terms — would be to say, "fuck you" and hang up the telephone.

He and I both knew that Packback had no other date to the Prom.

Meandering around the Clark Street bridge, gazing nostalgically at the dark Chicago River on which I'd spent countless hours as a tour boat deckhand in a simpler stage of life, my next phone call was to Kasey. The question that loomed:

What are the shareholders going to think?

In other words:

What have we dragged all these people into?

The esteemed community in our corner now felt like the overweight boulder on my back. It wasn't supposed to be this way. This wasn't how our fairy tale was supposed to play out.

Over the years, with the unfathomable fall of my beloved Chicago Bulls, came the unlikely rise of Packback. Or at least of Packback's promising, bright public reputation.

We'd become the stars of Illinois State University at age twenty-two.

Graced the cover of Chicago Crain's Magazine at age twenty-five.

And in the strangest worlds-collide manner imaginable, I'd transformed into my own unique flavor of differentiation as the *Ball Boy on Shark Tank*.

The protagonist isn't supposed to drown after a rebound.

Chapter 7

Hundred Twenty Dollar Minnows

Four years earlier. Fall 2013.

I was whizzing up Grand Street on my bicycle, headed home to Wicker Park, when my phone started buzzing.

Brock Kirby

Whoa.

He's actually calling me back?!

In the eighteen months since he'd confidently forecasted my illustrious future career as a Taco Bell franchisee during his campus visit, my great white whale had become elusive. I nearly fell off my hand-me-down rusted red Schwinn as I scrambled to answer the phone, feet still skidding on the ground as I spoke:

"Hello, this is Mike," I huffed.

"Hey Mike," replied Kirby, "what's up?"

"Hey Brock! How ya doing?"

"Good, I'm loving Boston, man! This is my place."

"Boston?"

"Yea, this is my place."

"Oh. What, uh, what are ya doing in Boston?"

"Mi— wait." he paused, presumably to look at his phone, "Oh. Is this Mike from *Packback?*"

"Yea!" I proudly confirmed.

"Oh, I thought I was calling…"

A different Mike.

His call was an accident. Oh well. I'll take what I can get.

We spoke for thirteen minutes, during which I had a hard time hearing Brock amidst the surround sound of a railway bridge, passing trucks, and the Chicago wind slapping me in the ear.

"So, remind me again, what's the elevator pitch?" he asked.

I gave him the pitch, again.

"Yea Mike, I don't know man, all that rental stuff is going away in six to twelve months," he said, "it's all going away."

I persisted.

"So how are you going to get the books?" Kirby asked, "You need to convince us and Pearson and all the publishers to give you books, right?"

"Yes."

"And how do you think you're gonna do that?"

"Well, that's what the pilot is setting out to prove," I explained, reminding him that McGraw-Hill had already provided us a dozen or so titles with which to conduct a limited pilot experiment at Illinois State University, "that we can attract the *used* book market students to daily digital rentals and act as a lead generator for full semester-long purchases…"

As I spoke, he remained as bored as ever with my party lines, but this time I had an ace in my pocket: a nationally televised cameo on his favorite TV show.

"We've been chosen for Shark Tank," I revealed, "would you like to be our 'phone-a-friend?'"

The ultimate honor.

Or so I thought.

"I don't think I want to be mentioned on Shark Tank" he demurred, "because I don't want to tell you that I don't believe in the business model on national TV."

Oh.

Yea that would be problematic.

Not the response I was hoping for.

We desperately needed those ISU pilot results to shine.

Kirby wished me good luck.

On September 15, weeks before the start of my seventh and final season as a Chicago Bulls ball boy, Kasey and I boarded the plane to Los Angeles.

When the plane touched down, we were picked up in a white van by a young guy with a long dark beard.

"So, you're from LA?" I asked him, fascinated to be in southern California.

"Yep, born and raised," confirmed Brent, "and I stuck around, for some reason. Most people tend to leave."

"Really? Seems like people are always leaving Chicago to *come* here, in our experience."

"Yea that's pretty much the norm," he agreed, "you won't find a lot of people that live here who grew up here. For any normal people who aren't chasing a dream, it's really kinda shitty."

Brent had stuck around, not for the glamor of his current temp gig as a go-fer on the set of Shark Tank, but rather in pursuit of his own dream: producing low-budget horror films.

"...I mean *really* low budget, like two hundred grand," he explained.

"Yea," I replied, "That's about our budget, too."

Brent drove us straight to a thrift shop, where our first assignment was to purchase their entire shelf of used books, the purpose being to create our set prop: a table overflowing with used textbooks.

As our journey through LA traffic inched along, Brent cracked opened his can of stories.

"Have you had a lotta weirdos you've dealt with for the show?" I asked.

"Ha!" he laughed, "Yes, definitely. In fact, just the other week..."

Brent had picked up a guy selling a pill that was going to cure hunger.

"My initial reaction was 'ok, well this is going to kill someone,'" Brent recalled, "and he tells me, 'you know how I know it works? Because I haven't eaten in ten days!'"

As went Brent's story, when the guy finally got to the Tank he was sweating profusely and looking ill. Then Mark Cuban made a show of calling him a snake oil salesman.

"That was probably the first guy I thought, 'holy shit, he's going to blow a gasket,'" recalled Brent, noting that while he doesn't *prefer* to see people fail, "sometimes you just have to laugh at some of the people."

We were, of course, about to join the ranks of those people—with as much or more of a chance of shredding our reputation as we had of filling our bank account. This was, after all, the number one family show on television enjoying the prime of its popularity. Eight million Friday night viewers tuned in weekly to witness the bright lights of America's most widely recognized entrepreneurial stage. Everybody and their great aunt Betty had a favorite episode.

The latest flavor of a well-laid formula for reality television.

Ask yourself, was it Kelly Clarkson who defined American Idol?

Or William Hung?

Come for the star. Stay for the blooper.

This wasn't just another pitch competition. This was *Shark Tank*.

And with a laughable hundred twenty dollars in revenue, we were minnows.

The morning of the pitch, I left our hotel room at 5:13 AM, went for a jog, and then walked around an empty dark parking lot practicing my answers to the questions we anticipated being grilled on from the Sharks.

I arrived back by 6:00 AM, ate a quick breakfast, showered, and rushed down to meet Kasey as the vans were loading. We rode along with a team of Jersey Shore-style dudes with a slick pitch for revolutionizing paint brush covers. Real nice guys, one of whom would later be arrested for felony cocaine trafficking charges.

Soon the van arrived at the studio.

On set, we were escorted via golf cart past a bunch of TV stuff such as the black Camaro from *Breaking Bad* and the building where they film *Wheel of Fortune*. No camera phones allowed. I'd been scolded for pulling mine out during a walk-through the day before.

We arrived at a trailer park and were shown to our trailer. Somebody on the set gave us an estimate that we'd be pitching around noon.

8:24 AM: entering our trailer, a lady said, "Hey guys! I'd like to grab one of you real quick for hair and makeup." I'd never done "hair and makeup" before. Kasey went first.

The next knock on the door: "Hi, I'm Laurel," she said, "the psychiatrist." We gathered with Laurel the Shrink for our pre-Tank psychiatric examination. Nailed it.

10:15 AM: another knock on the door. "Just to let you know," said the intern, "the second pitch has started."

11:05 AM: the intern knocked again. "Third pitch has started," they informed us. "Pitch four is already down there, so, probably in about twenty minutes we'll have you guys down there."

11:08 AM: a loud commotion rang out as the guys in our neighboring trailer returned from the Tank, whooping and hollering and high-fiving each other. Despite the LA heat, they all wore long fur hoods designed in the style of various animals. "Spirit Hoods," they were called. The scantily clad young ladies accompanying them were also wearing the hoods, if not much else.

"You guys were so awesome!" exclaimed one of the young ladies, "You got an offer, but you just didn't want it."

"They loved *you guys!*" replied one of the guys, "They were like 'we want more girls!'"

As the final minutes approached, I sat outside of the trailer on a plastic chair, flipping through my homemade paper flashcards like a high school kid taking one last desperate stab at cramming for an exam.

Somebody approached.

"You guys are up next."

Next thing I knew we were escorted to the pre-pitch room as former NFL lineman Bubba Baker and his daughter entered the Tank to pitch their baby back ribs company to the Sharks. On the door of the waiting room was a peculiar sign:

Shark Bait

Kate, the animated TV producer who'd selected our application months prior, joined us in the Shark Bait room. Reeling with enthusiasm, Kate wore a Spirit Hood during her pump-up speech.

Bubba Baker and his daughter finished their pitch.

You're up.

Kate led us to the double doors. It was a fake entryway leading to a fake living room. Just a television studio set. But when the doors opened, the bright lights and the Sharks facing us were all real.

Adrenaline pulsed through my veins.

Kasey and I walked up to the piece of blue tape on the floor that we'd been instructed to stand at. Stopped. Waited for fifty seconds while the camera crew snapped their still shots as we smiled and stared silently at the Sharks.

And then, when the producer gave the word…

Showtime!

By the time we arrived back at the trailer, reality didn't feel real.

Did that seriously just happen?!

What a rush. It had all the elements. Kasey and I high-fived. We hugged. We laughed about that stuff Mr. Wonderful had said, relating the nature of textbook publishers to his condition of baldness. That wise crack Daymond made about our matching outfits. That thing I said to Mark Cuban about stalking him last NBA season as he sat on the trainer's table while I was on ball boy duty in the Mavericks' locker room.

And how about Kasey at the end there?!

HA! Dude.

Within minutes, Laurel the Shrink arrived at the door for our post-Tank psychiatric examination. Nailed it again.

The rest of the afternoon was a blur.

We devoured the complimentary barbeque meal offered by the crew. Said one last goodbye to the Hollywood set. Boarded our chariot back to the new post-Tank hotel where we'd be separated from the other pre-Tank contestants.

Ate a late-night dinner across the street at Denny's.

Laying in our hotel beds that night, adrenaline still too high to sleep, Kasey and I watched some random movie called *Stand Up Guys*. The movie had one good line. A phrase that we'd soon adopt for our own purposes.

"What time is it?" asked Christopher Walken.

"I don't know," replied Alan Arkin, "what time *is* it?"

"It's time," chimed in Al Pacino, "to kick ass, or chew gum. And guess what?

Christopher Walken completed his sentence:

"I'm all outta gum."

Our version, which I'd soon print out and Scotch tape to the wall of our sublet office cubicle back home in Chicago, had a slight remix:

It's time to sign publishers or chew gum.

And we're all outta gum.

I felt like my life would never be the same. Like I'd stepped into a movie. Like this couldn't possibly be my reality. And due to the heavy NDAs, we couldn't leak a word about it until the episode aired.

Not to *anybody.*

Upon landing back in Chicago, the day before my twenty-fourth birthday, my dad picked me up from the airport.

"So...?" he inquired with a look.

Without taking a breath, I spilled all the juicy beans.

Chapter 8

Glory in a Bottle

Six months later, our episode finally aired.

March 21, 2014.

Over two hundred people, including a photographer and a reporter from the Chicago Tribune, crammed into the auditorium of Chicago's 1871 entrepreneurship center for our long-awaited episode viewing party. As went most aspects of my life in those days, the event itself was concocted for the sake of manufacturing artificial leverage against the textbook publishers. But nobody knew about that hidden agenda.

They just figured we were trying to make grandma proud.

With two hundred sets of eyes peeled to the auditorium projector screen, the second-to-last segment of the episode began.

A suit clad man of about thirty years old walked up the plank. He appeared polished, like a businessman, albeit one flaw: his dark hair was a scrambled mess.

"Hi Sharks, my name is Max Valverde, I'm from Boston, Massachusetts," he proudly declared, "and I'm the creator of *Morning Head*."

The number one family show in America took a detour into lude humor as Robert replied, "of *what?!*"

Mark Cuban grabbed his own head, laughing.

Daymond looked up, gesturing an imaginary "ahh."

Barbara replied with a sarcastic, "of course."

Upon sprinkling water into a diaper-like head-cap, putting it on his head, and wetting away his messy hair, Max from Boston wrapped up his opener. The pitch concluded with Max telling the Sharks that the best move they'll have made all year was "getting Morning Head."

Nobody bought it.

"This qualifies as poo poo on a stick," concluded Kevin O'Leary, "I'm out."

And with that, the episode's final segment began. Cheers erupted inside the auditorium as the projector screen displayed Kasey and me walking the plank.

Next up, is an affordable study tool for starving students.

Showtime.

After stating our names, and the deal on the table — two-hundred-thousand-dollars for ten percent equity — Kasey kicked us off:

"Sharks, let me ask you all a question. Do you remember what it was like, to be a college student?" He tugged at his blue unzipped hoodie. "Well Sharks, there's been a serious epidemic on the rise since your college days. And it's the cost of textbooks."

Kasey hand motioned towards the table next to us, which was overloaded with the pile of used books that we'd emptied out of the LA thrift shop and hauled around in a white van with Brent, the bearded, low budget horror filmmaker. Prominently displayed above the mess of books was a tablet on which glowed the Packback Books logo.

Behind the tablet was a large TV screen.

My head turned to address Mark Cuban.

"Hey Mark," I said, "did you know that since the time when you hung up your Hoosier hat, textbook prices have risen *eight hundred and twelve* percent?!"

"In fact," added Kasey, "the students are even *dropping out* of their courses in order to avoid the book costs."

"They are compromising their education!" I proclaimed, "but that's not the worst that can happen."

I pointed two fingers at the Sharks.

"Take a look at this" I said, now pointing at the TV screen.

Cue the cartoon animations.

A narrator's voice overtook the auditorium.

When you buy textbooks from the bookstore, you end up broke. When you end up broke, you have to get a job cleaning windows on campus. When you clean windows on campus, you look in and see parts of your professor you wish you hadn't.

The animated character, a college student standing on a window-washing pully, accidentally peeped on an elderly white-chest-haired man standing towel-clad in a bathroom. The window washing student made a disgusted noise and fell backwards, spilling his water bucket.

…When you see things you wish you hadn't, you fall off a ten-story building. When you fall off a ten-story building, you wind up in a full body cast and can't lug your expensive books to class. When you can't lug your expensive books to class, you sadly flunk out of college. And when you flunk out of college, you end up back in your mom's basement eating cookies on the couch in a onesie. …Don't end up eating cookies on the couch in a onesie. Use Packback Books.

Kasey and I finished the opening pitch by explaining how Packback's pay-per-use eTextbook website worked.

Then it was the Sharks' turn.

"You're walking right into my space…" opened Kevin O'Leary, which prompted a further tutorial from me about how the model works.

"So, Mike," asked Robert, "I'm going to assume that if you're in this business, you have a deal with the largest publishers in that space?"

Kasey and I replied in chorus:

"We have a deal with *one* of the largest."

I neglected to mention the nature of the phone call I'd had with the charismatic President of that one publisher weeks before flying out to LA.

"But why wouldn't one of the big guys just do this?" asked Daymond, "It's their property you're renting out anyway."

"Yes, eTextbooks are being sold. They've been around in the marketplace for around eight years," replied Kasey, "they're being rented by a semester for approximately a hundred, hundred fifty dollars per book."

"But you're doing it differently, the only difference being you're doing it by the day?" asked Barbara.

Kasey corrected her pedestrian simplicity:

"We're introducing a micro-transaction into this fragmented—"

Mark Cuban cut him off.

"You're pay-per-view."

We agreed.

More back-and-forth discussion occurred. *Margins. Average number of rentals.* The usual Shark Tank Economics 101 song and dance.

Then Kevin O'Leary, aka Mr. Wonderful, brought us all back to the moldy brick wall at hand:

"You have *no* exclusivity with these publishers, right?" he asked, "Because I've worked with these guys for over a decade, ok? They don't give exclusivity."

He was, of course, dead right.

More discourse.

The impossible threat of Amazon…

Students' average money spent on course materials…

The used book market…

"…the publisher didn't get a *dime* of that money," exclaimed Kasey.

"Are you telling me my kids are only looking at their textbooks *four* times a semester?!" asked Robert.

Damn right.

Daymond was the first to drop.

"I didn't go to college and I'm dyslexic so I can barely read," he explained, "I don't have any knowledge of this business. I'm out."

Logical.

Barbara croaked next.

"…I admire your persistence," she complimented us, "but I think you're gonna have a heck of a hard time, and I can't *imagine* all of the publishers going along for the ride. …I'm out."

Spot on.

Then Kevin O'Leary provided the keynote lecture of the episode:

"Guys, I like what you're doing, ok. I know your industry inside and out. I have *personally* negotiated deals with all of those publishers for over a decade. I will give you one small piece of advice: it'll take you a lot longer than you think to get the deals with those guys," he declared. "And while it sends a tingle through my spine to get back into the educational market, which is where I made the bulk of my net worth, I can't go back there," concluded the bald man, "If I walked into those offices again, I'd rip the *rest of my hair* out."

Kasey refuted Kevin by explaining something about Redbox, Netflix, and iTunes not being overnight successes either. O'Leary was undeterred.

"…it's important that you're young," he said, "cause by the time you finish with the educational publishers you'll be very old, ok? And I'm not saying it's not a noble pursuit. I have spent *thousands* of hours in their offices."

He pointed his right index finger at us.

"You will have no hair."

Then back at himself.

"You will both look like me when this is over. "

Then back at us.

"I am out."

A beautiful gift!

Mr. Wonderful, delightfully playing the role of the bad guy, had just voiced what everybody was already thinking. The thing that, in our endless act of publisher diplomacy, we couldn't say ourselves. By accurately mocking their snailish timidity, he'd set the stage for us to publicly defend the honor of our longed-for textbook publishing partners.

The camera shot to me.

"Here's what we think it takes," I began, "it takes the *right* contacts. When we find the right individuals within the organization, things click."

Camera panned to Mark Cuban, nodding his head. But before Mark could validate my publisher patriotism, Robert interjected.

"…everything in life is a gut feel." he said, "I just don't share your vision for this product. I'm out."

We thanked him for his time.

"…who's left?" asked Robert, "Mark?"

Cuban confirmed with a nod.

Dramatic music filled the auditorium.

The cameras flashed back and forth as we stared at each other.

Then Mark Cuban spoke.

"Ok, I like the concept. I mean I'm already in tech ed," he said, "but, ten percent, it isn't enough. And I want you guys to come back to me. What's the most equity I can get? How? And how much?"

Commercial break.

Oh, the suspense!

Our packed auditorium crowd cheered in anticipation. Seated front row center, we stretched our legs.

A photographer from The Chicago Tribune snapped a photo of Rishi Shah, a favorite young mentor of mine, standing up from his third-row seat next to a smiling Alan Matthew and Packback Board Member Mark Achler, excitedly leaning over my shoulder to show me his phone.

Twitter was erupting with talk of Packback Books.

A flurry of noise and side dialogue swept through the auditorium during commercial break. Then all went quiet again.

When the episode returned, Kasey and I were standing in an apparent stare down with Mark Cuban.

"You can talk," said Cuban.

We walked back into the hallway, a classic ingredient of any good Shark Tank episode. The height-of-suspense moment wherein, if not for that one troublesome detail regarding his lack of belief in our business model, we might otherwise have phoned Brock Kirby.

As Kasey and I conversed, Mark Cuban and Kevin O'Leary engaged a side dialogue in which Mr. Wonderful doubled down on his warning regarding the problematic nature of textbook publishers.

When we returned to the Tank, I kicked us off:

"Mark, we agree with what you're saying. We really value you as an investor. We want you to be very much vested into Packback's growth. We would like to offer you *seventeen and a half* percent for two hundred thousand dollars."

The counteroffer flashed up on the screen.

Implied pre-money valuation: $1,142,857.

Mark Cuban grabbed a pen to jot something down in his notepad. After a dramatic-music-induced pause, he spoke:

"What about, two hundred fifty thousand for twenty percent?"

Implied pre-money valuation: $1,000,000.

It hit the target valuation number that we'd concluded the night before in an email thread with our investor and board member, Howard Tullman. Camera flashed to Kasey and me. As a smile hijacked my poker face, upon realizing that we'd just landed our dream deal, Kasey spoke up on instinct:

"Would you do, would you be willing to do, *two* hundred thousand dollars, for the twenty percent?" he asked.

Implied pre-money valuation: $800,000.

The world froze for a moment.

Camera panned to a smirking Kevin O'Leary. Then to Barbara, who exclaimed, *"What?!"* The counteroffer numbers flash on the screen as her face burst into an open mouth laugh.

Same equity stake, for fifty grand *less cash* than what Cuban had offered.

It was a content producer's dream: Kasey had just committed a nationally televised math blunder with all the money on the line!

"Yes!" replied Mark Cuban, looking up from his notebook with his index fingers pointed at us.

Kasey and I both froze for a second as the math hit us.

"No." I replied, as the Sharks were all partaking in the laughter, "No that's not—"

Cuban put his notebook down and stood up to come shake our hands on the surprise new terms of the deal. On instinct, my hand flapped around in a dismissive gesture.

"…No, no, sit down, sit down, sit down!" said the Chicago Bulls Ball Boy to the Dallas Mavericks Team Owner in front of eight million Friday night viewers.

Smiles. Laughs.

Kasey clarified what he meant.

Mark conceded to the original deal.

Robert said something to the tune of "let's hit the rewind button on that."

I shook Mark Cuban's hand.

Kasey gave him a hug.

We exited the Shark Tank as our episode came to an end.

The auditorium erupted.

When the roaring applause finally subsided, Kasey and I took our seats on stage alongside ContextMedia CEO Rishi Shah who MC'd our post-episode audience discussion.

We sat on high-top chairs which naturally displayed our footwear. I was wearing a beat-up old pair of black Nike running shoes with lime green laces. The hand-me-downs gifted to me two summers earlier from Tim Grover.

Rishi kicked us off with a question:

"How do you feel *right* now? How do you feel?!"

"Yea I mean, we're totally on fire right now," replied Kasey, "but the biggest thing, of why we were ever so excited to go on the show in the first place, is when we had this vision of three-to-five-dollar digital textbooks, it was always a no brainer for students… anytime we would speak in front of a group of students, not only would they say 'hey you know this concept is awesome' or would adults say 'I wish I had this when I was in college,' but students would go so far as to rally behind us and say 'how can I help when you're at Michigan State University?'"

Cheers erupted in agreement.

Rishi smiled and nodded to the crowd.

"So now to be in front of literally *eight* million viewers nationwide," continued Kasey, "I have no idea, to be honest, what to expect."

The night before, Rishi and his co-founder Shradha Agarwal had hosted a small dinner for entrepreneurs, which gave us some time together to strategize how best to leverage this discussion for publisher-facing messaging. Having invited every publisher contact we'd ever made to the viewing party, Rishi knew exactly where this event needed to go.

"So, one of the points, probably the toughest point that came up on the pitch, was publishers are hard to work with," he recapped, "what do you make of that? How has it been working with publishers?"

I grabbed the mic.

Time to sing an onstage love song to the textbook publishers.

"Yeah, so …even when we won first place in our business plan competition as college students… they said basically 'good luck, you got a lotta energy, but you're never going to be able to work with these major publishers.'"

Hey, I'm not the one saying that textbook publishers suck, they were the ones saying it.

My love song continued:

"…what we found is the industry is in a *revolution*. So, the companies that are typically, you know, sort of old-fashioned companies, they're hiring former entrepreneurs, they're hiring technology leaders, very innovative thinkers. And if you can get through to those people, just like we do to investors, right, obviously it might take a few phone calls as people are busy, but when we find the *right* project sponsor…"

Time to pay homage to Brock Kirby's D-Word.

"…I mean basically there's a guy at McGraw-Hill, they were the first major learning company to give us a shot, right? They said, 'Well, we support entrepreneurship, we'll give you a shot.' We cold-called the President of McGraw-Hill when we were in college."

Murmur seeped from the audience. Rishi fueled it with an eyebrow-raised smile back at the crowd. Somebody chuckled and remarked, "wow," as I continued to tell the story of Kasey's cold call and Kirby's campus visit.

The story was always a hit.

Those kids are fearless.

"…he stayed in a little motel and he spent two days with us, right? So, this is the top of the food chain for these learning companies, and he just showed us that, you know, I'm going to believe in entrepreneurship."

Unmentioned was the heart melting thing that had happened between Brock Kirby and Mark Cuban a couple of months after we returned from LA.

And just how dire it had rendered our situation.

But for now, it was Shark Tank story time.

Rishi looked at Kasey.

"What happened when they went to break??" he asked with a smile, "Kasey, tell us about your negotiation…!!"

After the discussion wrapped up, a long line of smiling people approached Kasey and me: friends, family, investors, and Chicago startup community colleagues.

Handshake after celebratory handshake.

Proud pats on the back.

Hugs.

We were living in March of 2014, celebrating a moment of glory that had been captured in a bottle back in September of 2013.

In that televised moment, we were victorious.

In the six untelevised months after it, some seriously un-victorious stuff went down. But none of our suddenly growing fanbase knew about that. How could they?

And while the collective hug from family and friends was heartwarming, it wasn't the objective of our event. As the celebratory handshake line waned, it appeared that we'd missed our hidden agenda target.

The publishers we invited apparently hadn't shown.

Then, nearing the end of the line, a middle-aged man whom I'd never met before appeared before me. A friend of Howard Tullman's.

"Mark Whitaker," he said, extending a hand, "Pearson."

Chapter 9

Shark Baits Whale

Four months earlier. November 18, 2013.

"Come on guys," said Chicago Bulls team captain Luol Deng to the ball boys, as the Charlotte Bobcats' coaching staff grew increasingly irritated on the other side of the pregame court, "somebody's gotta go down there."

Eight weeks had passed since I shook Mark Cuban's hand. In the meantime, I was televised pumping a fist in the background of the Bulls' Halloween night home opener as Derrick Rose capped off his highly anticipated return with a game winning floater over Tyson Chandler to beat the Knicks.

The Bulls were back in business.

And while the blank white envelope that my boss handed me after each game still contained thirty-five bucks' cash, my backpack now contained a printed copy of a quarter-million-dollar term sheet from the owner of another team.

I'd been keeping it on hand given the frequent visits made to our attorney's office where we took our calls with Mark Cuban's legal team, after which I'd ride my bicycle over to the United Center on game nights. Given the sensitivity of the document, of course, I buried the backpack securely in the homogenous pile of ball boy crap that occupied the back corner of the laundry room next to the washing machines.

But the Charlotte Bobcats didn't know or give a damn about any of that.

They just wanted their balls rebounded.

Being title contenders again, I intended to preserve my premium rebounding services for the Bulls side, so I ignored Luol Deng's plea. Besides, a third ball boy, perhaps the laziest pre-game rebounder in Chicago Bulls history and a grown man of equal tenure to me as we both entered our seventh season as adult ball boys, had just arrived, tardy as usual.

It was on him to go over to the Bobcats side. Not me.

But what my colleague lacked in hustle he made up for in the sheer audacity of his stubbornness. He knew what awaited him on the other side: to be a lone rebounder. Two hours of nonstop chasing.

It was the classic game of chicken that defined our occupation:

Who can avoid doing the right thing for the longest?

The kind of thing ball boy career advancements are made of.

Alas, I capitulated.

Shaking my head, I ran down to the other side of the court. When I got there, the exceptionally large Charlotte Bobcats coach who'd been hollering for a rebounder was shaking his head, too. In an annoyed half-laugh, he expressed his displeasure with my delayed arrival.

"They got three, and we can't get *one?*" he lamented.

"Sorry guys," I replied, with an annoyed head nod toward my colleagues, "high maintenance."

Then I noticed the name etched onto his shoes, which prompted me to do a double take on his face.

Oh! So that's why Luol Deng cared to intervene.

It was Patrick Ewing.

The NBA Hall of Famer was employed as an assistant coach for the team now owned by his former rival, Michael Jordan.

I hustled like hell to keep a ball in Ewing's hands.

Such was reality as my final season as a ball boy overlapped with my coming of age as an entrepreneur. A textbook publisher conference call here. An investor pitch there. A debate with Mark Cuban's lawyers in the morning. A subtle reprimand from Patrick Ewing in the afternoon.

The Bulls beat the Bobcats as I surveilled the courtside seats for recognizable angel investors and gazed off at the owner's skybox wondering what Reinsdorf might be discussing with the group of Chinese delegates he was hosting. Stationed behind the visitors' side bench, throughout the game, I formed a bond with the sociable equipment manager of the Charlotte Bobcats who spoke to me about how I might one day become a trusted equipment manager.

At 5:01 AM the next morning, I punched the *send* button on my first ever email directly to Mark Cuban.

Despite the eight weeks that had passed, our deal was far from done, stuck in a knot of attorney arm-wrestling matches over details that I couldn't care less about. Our main source of communication after the Shark Tank handshake was not Mark but rather a business manager type of guy named Stephen. Nice guy and all, but he wasn't Mark Cuban.

And our startup survival tale was increasingly in need of a Shark.

McGraw-Hill was not behaving.

What began with Brock Kirby's glorious visit to campus eighteen months prior, had devolved into a corporate web of timidity, a flavor of sluggishness that threatened to kill us. The game to be played was as follows:

1. Take the dozen or so titles made available to us at Illinois State University for daily rentals and promote them to the slim selection of relevant students.[6]

2. Students rent the books on PackbackBooks.com in 24-hour increments as needed (which is to say, when it came time to cram).

3. Survey & measure those students, package the results into a flashy PDF, and show it to McGraw-Hill to prove that our customers would have otherwise bought or rented *used* books from which McGraw-Hill receives no revenue.

Net positive fall semester revenue impact evidenced by the PDF, we then expected to simply gain approval for an extended list of McGraw-Hill's thousands of textbooks titles in the spring semester and proceed to spread the gospel of Packback Books to the masses.

Simple, right?

Tell that to our insider at McGraw-Hill.

The fate of our title list expansion approval was trapped inside of a fuzzy knot of corporate yarn—as depicted by our insider, a college friend named Aubrey, whom Kirby had hired after the dinner we'd curated for him during his original campus visit:

---

6. Given our narrow list of titles, only a small selection of classes was deemed relevant, and thus broad marketing efforts were futile. That meant we had to go through the professors. Adding to the array of forces opposing the existence of a daily textbook rental option, professors of our own alma mater turned out to be less than thrilled about PackbackBooks. com. Nor was our campus bookstore manager, who issued us a cease-and-desist letter for the "Your Bookstore is Robbing You" flyers we'd posted around campus to garner student attention. It took a stealthy effort of sneaking into a classroom or two to even get in front of the students to inform them of the McGraw-Hill pilot, but that's another story for another day.

Chase, a little dog in Indiana, had spoken with Derek, a seemingly random dog in Colorado, but Derek still had to talk to Grant, a big dog in Illinois. While Chase was said to be our project sponsor, it was Grant and Derek who had to decide whether to expand the pilot.

Per Chase, that decision "likely requires some input from Kirby."

So, Chase was waiting to hear back from Derek. Derek was awaiting an analysis of viable backlist titles from Aubrey. And, unbeknownst to either Chase or Derek, Kasey was actively backchanneling with Aubrey to ensure that the analysis looked favorable for Packback.

And then, if that wasn't confusing enough for you, there was also the question of a broader "front list" e-textbook catalogue that would be deemed too valuable for daily rental access but that we might distribute in the "standard" semester-long fashion just like any other eTextbook vendor.

On that topic, there was a woman named Diana, a big dog in New York, who would need to weigh in. And Diana wouldn't be able to weigh in until the occurrence of an all-dogs "committee meeting" in mid-January which would determine McGraw-Hill's "new set of standards for e-book retailers."

Woof.

All told, not counting Diana's faceless committee, we were at the mercy of at least six stakeholders, paralyzed in this web of indecision.

And the weather forecast was getting cloudier.

"I'll be straight up with you," said Chase Maddox on a recent check in call, "there are still some concerns. Not about you guys, but around the daily rentals, period... We want to keep it at a pilot so that when Amazon and Google come knocking on the door, we can say 'it's just a pilot with Packback at limited schools and we're only doing it for the data.'"

January classes were starting in a matter of weeks. If we missed the spring semester expansion window, it'd be *nine months* until we'd get another crack at a pilot test in the fall 2014 semester. That's about a decade in seed-stage startup years.

We had neither the patience nor the financial runway for a nine month wait.

Hence, desperation is the unwed mother of boldness.

I decided to breach the Shark Tank NDA in a Hail Mary attempt at Brock Kirby. Leap past the middle management dog pile once and for all. Electrify the White Whale. After all, as would later be declared by our project sponsor, "if Brock wants to do a pilot, we're done."

But the whale was elusive.

Weeks prior, I'd attempted to net him by cashing in on his long ago *serious* promise to take me to a Knicks game at Madison Square Garden. I emailed a sampler of the team's schedule to his assistant and offered to fly out for whichever game worked best for him. No luck. As if trained to play the role of calendar bad cop, Kirby's assistant doubled down on how busy he was:

…No one would believe Brock's calendar—it keeps getting busier. I keep thinking time will open in the future, but it gets tighter—often double and triple booked! As much as I know he would love to get to a game with you, I don't see an opening coming up which is sad. I'm surprised he gets to see his family!

This time I pulled out my phone.

Having discovered that he was in Chicago for a private event hosted by some other guy that I *sort of* knew, and, like an obsessed stalker, wanting Kirby to know that I knew where he was, I figured at minimum I'd leave him a voicemail and hope for a cab ride call back.

Two dials in, he answered.

"This is Brock."

"Hey Brock! This is Mike Shannon, from Packback."

"Hey Mike Shannon from Packback, what's up?"

"So, I wanted to give you a call, I heard from one of my contacts at Patina Solutions that you were giving a sales presentation this morning and I was actually trying to see if I could listen in, but I assume it's over now, uhh, are you still in Chicago?"

"Yea we just finished up at [the hotel]. I'm still here but getting ready to leave," he replied. "So who do you know at Patina? You seem to be everywhere, man. I like that about you."

I gave him an update on the pilot results at Illinois State, outlined my understanding of the project's next steps, and name dropped a recent conversation with a private equity executive named Antoine who sat on McGraw-Hill's Board of Directors.[7]

"Yea, I talked to Antoine," replied Kirby, "he called me and said he was going to talk to you. I told him I like the hell out of you, ha! Which is probably why he got on the phone at all."

Our conversation carried on.

---

7. McGraw-Hill was, at the time, owned by a private equity group. Kasey had garnered some intel on the PE guys from, of all places, one of our angel investor insurance executives (for whom Kasey and Nick had worked as summer interns) in Bloomington-Normal, IL. That guy happened to oversee the large insurance provider's investment portfolio and thus was routinely pitched by PE groups to invest in their funds. He handed Kasey the McGraw-Hill board member.

"The thing for me," said Kirby, "is that I still don't know how McGraw makes any *money* on it, other than that I like the hell out of you. I'd like to see the economics of what happened at Illinois State and how McGraw made *money*."

"Yea absolutely," I replied, "so, we have all of that and we've reported with Grant, Derek, Chase—"

Kirby cut me off.

"What you really want to have happen is for Grant and Derek to come to me and say, 'hey Brock we think there's really some money to be made here, this is what they did at Illinois State.'"

"Ok, so I was under the impression that Grant had touched base with you after we went over the results?" I asked.

"No no, see what you've got to understand, well, you *do* understand because you're keeping up with all the shit, with a large company there's four hundred fifty people. People don't follow up on stuff."

"Ok, well that's good to know. Yes, I can send you a very simple outline of the economics and what it did for McGraw-Hill. I think we have everyone pretty much on the same page…"

Yawn. Boring. All this talk of "pilot results analysis" was going nowhere. White noise flowing in one ear and out the next. Rambling on like an undifferentiated loser, I was losing him. He himself had taught me better than that. So, finally, I shifted gears, stepped into a dim-lit conference room, and shut the door for privacy.

Time to show Brock Kirby my D-word.

"Sooo, then the other thing, is what happened when we went on Shark Tank," I said, "we accepted a deal with Mark Cuban."

Light switch.

"Well congratulations," Kirby replied, with newfound interest in remaining on the phone with me, "Mark Cuban is the perfect partner for you guys because he has a tech background. So, what's the deal?"

"It's two hundred fifty thousand and he'll have a twenty percent stake in the company."

"Ok. Well," started Kirby, "if you were *really* smart, you'd get me tickets to a Bulls-Mavs game and set up a meet—"

"December 28th!" I cut him off, already aware of the schedule as I was on the ball boy roster to work that game, "Are you in town December 28th?"

I finally had something he wanted.

"I'm in Vegas for a UFC fight with my son," he replied.

"Alright well the Mavs game is on December 28th, but—"

He cut me off.

"Ok well here lemme tell you, I can afford my own tickets, and I travel all the time. The *best* thing you can do, and this is my advice on how you can really leverage your network," Kirby explained, "is to tell Mark that the *President* of McGraw-Hill would love to meet him to hear it from Cuban... tell him Shark Tank is the favorite show in his household, and he loves him."

Kirby was animated now.

"...By the way, this could get you *bought*. That's the best thing that Mark Cuban can do for you and the best thing for himself as an investor, if he can get McGraw-Hill fully on board, which right now we're not. I don't know anything about it other than I like the hell out of you guys."

Then he rolled up his coaching sleeves.

"...this is how you present it. You say: 'hey Mark, the *President* of McGraw-Hill is going to be in Dallas in March and April. He wants to meet you for a few minutes and hear your take on Packback. He mentioned it could be an acquisition for McGraw."

As odd as the sudden acquisition potential sounded, I loved every word of what I was hearing.

"This is me giving you advice on how to leverage your network," concluded Kirby, "this is how you do it."

Say no more, big man.

I got this.

Chapter 10

Checkmate

Mark Cuban replied to my email right away.

In fact, not only did he reply to my request to "play ball with us" in a coercive lobbying effort on the President of McGraw-Hill Higher Education, but he also upped the ante. Beyond offering to meet him any time, Cuban rolled out the red carpet by inviting Kirby to attend a Shark Tank taping as a behind-the-scenes private guest of Mark Cuban.

Unbelievable!

Mark Cuban's involvement secured, I sent him a theatrical email on a new thread, designed for Brock Kirby to be looped into after Mark replied, which wrapped up with a heap of praise on Kirby:

…Brock Kirby is without a doubt one of the most innovative leaders and influencers in the higher education publishing space. I think you will enjoy meeting him if possible. Do you think we can work this out?

Cuban replied as planned, and then I looped Brock Kirby into the thread for an introduction. Again, Mark replied immediately:

From: Mark Cuban

Brock

Great to connect with you. Feel free to reach out any time. I'm obviously a huge fan of packback and I am happy to answer any questions about my support and interest

And re Shark Tank we shoot in June and Sept, so it's a ways off, but when we start up would love to take you behind the scenes

Have a great holiday and keep in touch

M

Having delivered his impossible request on a silver platter, I then shot over a separate email to Kirby, CC'ing a few of his executives, that dropped our "ask" on the table:

…We had two good conversations this morning with Chase Maddox and Aubrey Lane. Aubrey is preparing a report for selection of the Packback titles for phase II pilot next semester. Sounds like Chase is awaiting a response from Derek Ritz and Grant Briggs. I know the national sales meeting is fast approaching and everybody is very tight on time. It would be extremely helpful if we could have a decision for extended pilot before the start of next semester. If you could possibly help expedite things in any way that would be greatly appreciated. Your meeting(s) with Mark Cuban will have much more context if we can execute on a true pilot with the requested 100 titles per campus.

It was a beautiful manifestation of all that Shark Tank stood for. The heavy-hitting Shark engaging combat with the Whale on behalf of the Minnows.

Mark Cuban was the real deal.

And having just brokered a relationship between a Shark and a Whale, I fancied myself a certified twenty-four-year-old power player. All that was left to do now was sit back and wait for McGraw-Hill's title list expansion to fall into my lap.

Checkmate.

With an eye glued to my inbox, I waited.

Waited some more.

Day turned into night which turned into more days.

I kept waiting.

Confusion turned into nerves which turned into *what the hell?*

Silence.

At the peak of our soap opera's suspense, Kirby did the one thing that I never imagined him capable of:

Nothing.

Days later. Bulls vs. Cavs.

Hungry after a two-hour pre-game rebounding session, I was standing in line for food in the media room of the United Center when my phone buzzed in my pocket. A text from Kasey.

I got that weird email from Chase today. Check your email and give me a call when you get a chance.

I checked it immediately.

Buried inside a paragraph of fluff, there it was:

The dagger.

… McGraw-Hill has chosen to take a pass on the opportunity to pilot 24-hour rentals at this time.

Face flush, heart sinking, mind racing, I politely asked the media room chef for an Italian beef sandwich with a side of chopped salad as I contemplated the email.

It made no sense.

What happened? Kirby had asked for the impossible—a personal meeting arranged between him and Mark Cuban. Within forty-eight hours, I delivered. Cuban upped the ante even further, rolling out the red carpet by inviting Kirby to be his personal guest at a Shark Tank taping.

Kirby had so confidently told me that *this could get you bought.*

Then he ghosted.

Not a word of reply to either of my emails.

And now this.

What …the fuck?!

My Great White Whale was officially dead in the water, and nobody else in the United Center knew or cared about it as Carlos Boozer scored nineteen points and Joakim Noah pulled down eighteen rebounds en route to a Bulls victory.

My eyes were watching a game of basketball, but all my mind could see was the collapse of a startup company.

McGraw-Hill was "out."

With that, we'd lose the leverage for acquiring any other publishers.

It'd be only logical for Mark Cuban to subsequently drop his yet-unsigned investment agreement, and for the Shark Tank producers to kill our episode before it ever aired.

This would be the death of Packback.

End of book.

Checkmate.

Chapter 11

The Ball Boy on Shark Tank

Of all the celebratory text messages that flooded my phone as Morgan and I walked out of the 1871 auditorium near midnight after Shark Tank aired, it was the one from Bulls trainer Jeff Tanaka that stood out:

Sooo, are you coming to work tomorrow?????

Absolutely.

Eighteen hours after appearing on national television shaking the hand of another team's owner, I was back in the Chicago Bulls' laundry room yanking a load of fresh towels out of the dryer.

That was, until the bosses summoned me to the trainers' room.

"You're the only ball boy in history to use the word 'monetize' in a sentence!" declared head trainer Fred Tedeschi, infinitely amused by our unusual pregame conversation about "monetizing backlist titles" and "combatting cannibalization from the used book market on behalf of textbook publishers."

By now, a small circle had gathered around me in the back corner of the trainer's room, at the same spot where Michael Jordan had once played quarters with his security staff.

"I haven't said five words to him in seven years," continued Fred, with a look to someone else in the circle. "He started talking last week and my jaw hit the floor."

Our prior week's conversation was an accident turned blessing.

In the weeks leading up to the Shark Tank airing, I'd been stealthily seeking small pockets of player interactions in attempts to ask them if they would Tweet about Packback when the episode aired. The hopeful NBA player Tweets were part and parcel to a strategy Kasey was architecting to get Packback to go viral and thus manufacture pressure on the textbook publishers. With only one pre-episode game remaining to secure the Tweets, I encountered a wrinkle to my clandestine operation.

Shark Tank???

It was a text from Mike Smetana, my since-retired visitors' side locker room vet who'd helped me get into rotation in my early days. Above the text was a snapshot of a TV displaying my face. A preview of next week's Shark Tank episode had aired. It wasn't long before the ball boys all knew.

Later that same afternoon, I was rebounding for Bulls guard Kirk Heinrich, passing the ball to Bulls assistant coach Mike Wilhelm. Had there been a metric to measure it, I'd confidently bet that Wilhelm, who'd become a genuine mentor to me over the years, would have ranked as the nicest man in the history of the NBA. Between passes, Coach Wilhelm gave me a funny look.

"Hey Mike," he said, "did you go on the Shark Tank?"

When I confirmed, yes, he shook his head as if to say *I knew it!*

"My son loves it," Coach Wilhelm explained, telling the story to Kirk Heinrich as Kirk continued shooting, "...So I'm sitting there watching it and at the end it shows short clips of next week's episode, and I said, *'holy shit* that's the ball boy Mike!'"

The sudden awareness made me nervous, as I hadn't yet secured all my player Tweets. Staying under the radar was becoming a game of limbo. By the time I stepped into the Bulls locker room for the post-game cleanup, that limbo bar had all but collapsed.

"Yo Shannonnnn," said my colleague, Kyle, as he wiped a towel to a Gatorade bucket alongside me, "it's getting around man. Even Tanaka knows. Did you tell him?"

"Ah shit, he knows?" I replied, putting my towel down, "I gotta go talk to him then."

"Yea I don't know, he came up to me and said, 'which ball boy is going on Shark Tank?'"

I had planned on telling Jeff myself, when the timing was right. Too late. I walked into the trainer's room to turn myself in.

"I guess word spreads fast," I said.

"So it's you?" asked Jeff, "What's happening? You're going on *Shark Tank?*"

Head trainer Fred Tedeschi, with whom I'd never had a single conversation in seven years, gathered around along with Director of Sports Performance, Jen Swanson. Nearly two decades prior, the tears of Michael Jordan had soaked the carpet beneath my feet as he clutched the game ball after the Bulls' 1996 Father's Day Championship. Now, the floor was mine.

"I started a company in college," I began, "we're essentially a platform for college students to rent digital textbooks in a pay-per-use model. So, basically, they can rent for a day at a time instead of wasting a ton of money on books that are barely used."

"That's smart," someone replied, as the others nodded their agreement.

"So let me ask you a question, and tell me if it came up," said Fred, playing the role of Shark for a moment, "what's to prevent a kid from buying it for a day and then ripping the whole book?"

Softball.

Come on, Fred, gimme something hard to sell.

"Yea that's a great question," I replied, "So first off, the industry wants to go digital, and so everyone faces that risk. We have what's called Digital Rights Management software…"

As my colleagues congregated down the hallway over shared post-game laundry duties, I dove into a technical explanation about DRMs for the bosses.

"This guy's smart," said Fred, giving Jeff a curious glance, "I mean, you look smart, with the glasses, but we kinda look at ball boys a certain way."

Fred twisted his hands and made a face like he'd just encountered a pile of stink. It was the most apt description I'd ever heard spoken aloud of the organizational status of the ball boys.

"So," one of them asked, "you told Cuban about your work as a ball boy, right?!"

Oh, did I ever.

"Yea, so, I'll just tell you guys, because I'm not sure if it's going to air." I began, "When the producers pick out your submission video and start working with you, they ask for anything that differentiates you which might make the show more interesting."

"Well *that's* a differentiator!" Jeff remarked.

"Right," I agreed, "and so I called Joe O'Neil to see if it'd be ok to say it."

"Suuuure!" said Fred, in a gruff Santa Clause-ish voice that imitated the Bulls' longtime gregarious Irish Ticket Sales Director, Joe O'Neil.

"Yes," confirmed Jeff, "the Bulls support entrepreneurship."

"Who knows," added Fred, "they might even put you up on Bulls TV."

"So let me tell you what happened," I continued, "When we were up there, I ended up saying, 'well Mark, you know we actually bumped shoulders in one of my side jobs.'"

Their eyes widened as I rendered my guilty plea to the most public violation in the history of Ball Boy Commandment Number Two.

"He got interested, and I said, 'throughout college I worked as a ball boy for the Chicago Bulls. And last year, I was working in the Mavs locker room when you came. I wanted to talk to you, but the Bulls ended up winning by about thirty points that night…'"

It was actually a twenty-three-point margin, but the rest of the story's details were accurate. The prior season, when the Dallas Mavericks came to town, I had the pregame visitor's locker room turf. Mark Cuban, who stepped off the team bus and walked past me as I approached to grab the luggage, sat on the trainer's table in the back of the locker room typing on his phone throughout most of the two-hour pregame time. It was to be my golden moment.

Don't be a chicken!
That's Mark Cuban right there!
Go pitch him about Packback!

But the Mavericks' training staff was within earshot, and if I got caught, they'd surely rat me out to the Bulls' training staff. So, there I stood, frozen at my fly-on-the-wall post inside of the Dallas Mavericks locker room, mind racing to perfectly craft my value proposition, as minutes slipped off the clock until I'd finally blown what I believed to be my only shot at pitching Mark Cuban.

Frustrated by the loss, Cuban headed straight for the exits after the game.

When I recalled the story for Mark during an unaired portion of our dialogue inside the Shark Tank, all the other Sharks had fun digging at him when I reminded Mark of the Bulls victory.

"That's either the smartest," remarked a laughing Fred Tedeschi, "or the *dumbest* fucking thing you did!"

Story time continued.

It was nearly eleven o'clock at night by the time we wrapped up.

Fred looked at Jeff.

"Yea, this is Bulls-wide," he concluded, instructing Jeff to send an email to the entire Chicago Bulls organization, "get it out tonight or early tomorrow morning. Especially if it's out there like that. This way we avoid it being 'hey there was a ball boy on Shark Tank! Why didn't we know about it??'"

Jeff agreed.

Then he looked at me.

"Hey, just remember, we gave you your start," he said, "we funded it, thirty-five dollars at a time!"

My bosses and I were the last to depart the empty locker room that night.

Fred extended a congratulatory handshake.

Jeff gave me a hug, and then sent me a text the next day:

We emailed the organization and are letting players know as well. May try to get some shout outs on Twitter...

Now, a week later, part-two of my story time with the bosses continued in the same spot. When it wrapped up, they each warmly congratulated me again.

"Alright," concluded Fred, aptly capturing the spirit of the situation, "now go get the shit out of my car. Ha ha!"

I was glad to do it.

Previously unimaginable green light secured, I'd come prepared for my pursuit. Stuffed into the pocket of my sweatpants was a thick wad of one-by-four-inch pieces of printer paper that I'd cut and glued to thick construction paper for enhanced sturdiness.

Bulls player Tweet scripts.

Joakim Noah had his full warmup gear on when I caught him in the hallway on his way to the court from the locker room. Awkwardly explaining my situation while inconveniencing his otherwise focused pre-game preparation process, I handed him a Tweet script:

"Broke college students tune in to Shark Tank..."

Joakim didn't like it.

"*Broke* college students?" he balked, "I can't say 'broke college students,' put them on blast like that. Come on man."

Though I tried to elaborate, he was right. It wasn't the appropriate Tweet for Joakim Noah. In a nervous scramble, I pulled the full wad out of my pocket, causing Joakim to make the sort of odd face that my odd mannerisms warranted.

"Damn," he remarked, as I shuffled through them like a deck of Pokémon cards, "how many of those you got?"

A lot. I had a *lot* of Bulls player Tweet scripts in my pocket that day.

And life had changed.

I now walked the underground halls of the United Center reborn as a mysterious new creature:

The Ball Boy on Shark Tank.

The remainder of the 2013-2014 NBA season was a rush of this new existence.

Bulls staff members whom I'd never met before introduced themselves to me.

Derrick Rose, when I caught him in the laundry room to discuss the Tweet operation, was curious about whether Mark Cuban had stayed involved with the investment. Indeed he had, I proudly reported back to D-Rose. A few weeks before the episode aired, Cuban was in Chicago for a speaking event and spent over an hour with us in a private meeting we held at Howard Tullman's office.

Separately, Rose's security guard poked his head into the wet room one game as I was tending to the Gatorade carts and jokingly asked me for a loan.

During a lull in pregame rebounding time, an assistant coach asked me, as a genuine clarification of how startup investments work, if Packback was trading on the NASDAQ.

Passing the Reinsdorf family in the post-game loading dock one evening, after being congratulated by the kids and applauded for the great idea, Bulls President Michael Reinsdorf asked me if I still needed the ball boy job. Then, with a nod to Kasey's now infamous blunder, he joked that "your buddy almost fucked it up there at the end."

Kasey's math error had the incidental effect of transcending us beyond the ordinary categories of Shark Tank contestants, resulting in a priceless double dip. We were simultaneously a winner and a blooper. As such, Kasey went viral on Reddit with an Ask Me Anything thread that surpassed fifteen hundred comments:

I'm a 23-year-old entrepreneur... I went on Shark Tank, accidentally counter-offered Mark Cuban $50K LESS than he offered me, and am fixing the broken textbook industry with my startup. AMA!!

Sam Smith, the New York Times bestselling author of *The Jordan Rules*, briefly interviewed me while the two of us stood outside of the visitor's locker room. Then he cited my Shark Tank appearance in his next Bulls newsletter.

It was all exhilaratingly strange. A fellow ball boy summed up the peculiarity of my newfound status by remarking that, "you know something weird's going on when [Bulls equipment manager] Ligs asks you, 'how's business?'"

My two worlds had collided.

And then they began communicating with each other.

An angel investor of ours, Chicago tech titan and University of Chicago Booth professor Mark Tebbe, stationed at his usual courtside seats near the Bulls bench where I'd been routinely sneaking over to deliver him personalized investor updates at halftime throughout the season, grabbed Bulls-side security guard Tony's attention during a game.

"Hey, you know where you could have seen this guy last week?" asked Tebbe, pointing playfully at me while I was working behind the Bulls bench, "He was on TV!"

Tony was, of course, already aware. My longtime security guard pals had all cheered on the episode while watching it at home with their families.

During a timeout of that same game, while standing on the court outside of the Bulls' huddle as Coach Thibs drew up a play, I made a hand signal to Tebbe in the motion of signing a document, conveying that I needed him to submit his signature of approval. After six long months since the Shark Tank handshake, we were finally nearing legal completion of Mark Cuban's investment.

In the three months since my White Whale had shockingly rolled over dead in the water, and all hope appeared lost, our Shark never dropped us.

Surreal new status aside, by the time the Milwaukee Bucks came to town on April 6th, former college hoops phenom Jimmer Fredette, now a Bulls reserve guard, remained the only player to Tweet about Packback.

I was working on the visitors' side, awaiting the arrival of Milwaukee's team bus. In the meantime, as was our custom, I provided a golf cart ride down the hallway to the eighty-four-year-old security anchor who guarded the front door of the Bulls locker room. His name was John Capps, but everybody just called him Capps. Been with the Bulls since Day One. Find any footage of Michael Jordan in the 90s, and you'll see Capps standing guard somewhere in the background.

In his heyday, the Marine veteran and former Chicago police officer was a beefed up badass. Nowadays, Capps had a bad back.

Upon arriving at the front door of the Bulls locker room, I jumped out of the golf cart to grab a fold-up chair for him out of the assistant coaches' room while Capps fiddled in his pocket for the unrequested fare that he always generously insisted on paying me for the ride.

"Capps, you're still over-paying me," I replied, as he stuffed the roll of three singles into my hand.

"Yeaaa well," grunted Capps, "when you're a billionaire, you can say 'hey that guy used to give me a dollar!' Ha ha ha!"

When I returned to the loading dock, I continued my conversation with another security guard, my friend Pat, who was also a former Chicago cop. Pat had long ago nicknamed me "Crash," ever since that one time when I accidentally let a golf cart crash into a fancy car that the Blackhawks had parked in the loading dock to keep it safe before they raffled it off at their next game. Whoops.

Pat loved to revisit that story. But right now, the story was Shark Tank, and Pat had watched the episode at home with all his kids.

As we spoke, my phone buzzed with an email from Mark Whitaker, the Pearson executive who had introduced himself to me at our episode viewing party. My subsequent chat with John had gone well, and now he was arranging for a meeting with another Pearson big dog named Bill Triant who happened to be flying in from New York City next week.

I confirmed the meeting with Pearson while seated at the wheel of my red golf cart, still conversing with Pat, as we both awaited the arrival of the Milwaukee Bucks. A few hours later, I'd go grab Mark Tebbe's courtside attention at halftime to invite him to that Pearson meeting as well, for extra fire power on our side of the table. Tebbe agreed to join. But for now, I had a mission to complete.

As all ball boys know, pregame visiting team bus duty coupled as prime turf for unsupervised interactions with Bulls players as they entered the stadium through the loading dock.

Shortly after I thanked Jimmer Fredette for his generous Tweet, in walked Chicago's favorite seven-footer. His long hair flowing loose without its signature ponytail, beard unkempt, and sweatpants tucked into his socks, I looked at him with a smile and a head tilt.

"Hey, so, can I get it?" I asked.

He looked at me sideways, then his eyes lit up and his head jerked back as if remembering something.

"Oh!" replied Joakim Noah, "I forgot!"

"It's cool jus—"

"Let's do it now," he said, reaching into his pocket.

"Ok yea let's do it now!" I agreed, "It's really just the '@ PackbackBooks' that's important."

As he pulled out his phone, something else caught his attention. Several members of the Noah family, particularly an elderly woman whom I assumed to be his grandmother, were waiting to greet him.

"Here," he said, handing me his phone, "you do it."

"Ok," I replied, somewhat nervous to be holding Joakim's iPhone 5, "I'll have you review it first."

"Cool" he said, then walked away to kiss his grandmother.

Hand shaky, eyes staring down at Joakim Noah's Twitter app home page that asked me *'what's going on?'*, I asked myself a different question:

How would Joakim Noah phrase this message, if he had actually watched our Shark Tank episode and was actually so randomly enthused by the textbook-rental segment that, weeks later, he burst into his first ever spontaneous Shark Tank Tweet?

Here's what came to mind:

Big shout to @packbackbooks for taking names on #sharktank for #affordable books

When Joakim reappeared, I handed him his phone.

"Here, is that ok?"

He paused for a moment, gave it a contemplative look, then concluded, "ok that's good."

Tap.

My man Joakim!

He continued walking towards the hallway.

"Hey but have you actually seen it?" I asked.

"No I haven't" he replied, still moving forward.

"But you know the show Shark Tank right?"

"Yea yea."

"Here I'll walk with you."

I hopped out of my golf cart to catch up to Joakim, but he still had family to meet with.

"Send it to me," he said, "you got my number?"

"No I don't."

"You got your phone on you?"

"Yea yea."

I pulled my phone out of my pocket.

"Here take down my number," he said, "it's ###-###-####"

"Ok cool got it." I confirmed, "I'll send you a link"

"Cool."

It was not lost on me that, with the addition of Joakim Noah's cell phone number to my address book, I had achieved the supreme ambition of a ball boy. This was *Flounder*-level territory, yet with an added spice of public flair. The stream of text messages that flowed into my phone throughout the remainder of the evening echoed one consistent theme:

Dude! Joakim Noah just tweeted about Packback!

And they were right. Technically speaking, the soon-to-be-named NBA Defensive Player of the Year *did* tap the button.

Just when I thought I'd experienced all the absurdity that I was going to see, Sharrod entered the back laundry room door after a game one evening.

"Hey Shannon," he said, "Steve Schanwald's looking for you."

Steve Schanwald?!

"He's looking for *me?*" I replied, confused.

"Yea," confirmed Sharrod, "he was asking around for who the ball boy on Shark Tank was."

Bulls' Executive Vice President of Business Operations, Steve Schanwald, was the business-side number two to team owner Jerry Reinsdorf. Six years prior, during my first season, at the encouragement of assistant coach Mike Wilhelm, I introduced myself to Schanwald while he sat courtside during pre-game warmups. In that brief interaction, I mispronounced his name and then never worked up the nerve to say hi to him again.

The following summer, like everyone else in Chicago, I watched Steve on ESPN, standing next to Dwayne Wade, when the fateful ping pong balls of the 2008 NBA Draft Lottery landed the Bulls the first pick of the draft that would bring home Derrick Rose. Months later, as a freshman at Illinois State, I heard a keynote speaker talk about the power of writing down goals and placing them somewhere visible. That night, the words "Executive Vice President of the Chicago Bulls" went up on my dorm room wall as a life goal.

At nineteen years old, I was looking to be the next Steve Schanwald.

Now, at twenty-four, Steve Schanwald was looking for me.

I was rebounding on the Bulls side during the next pre-game when he walked by.

"Hi Steve!" I said, uncharacteristically abandoning my rebound station as I approached him with an extended hand.

"Hi" he replied, confused as to why a ball boy had gone rogue to engage an on-court networking conversation.

"Sharrod mentioned you were looking for me." I explained, "I'm Mike Shannon, I was on Shark Tank."

"Oh yea that was you?!" exclaimed Steve, "Congratulations…"

At the conclusion of our brief reintroduction, he reached into his suit pants pocket, and I reached into my sweatpants pocket. Upon swapping business cards, I promised to send him an email to schedule a meeting.

My final frontier was set. Before my carriage turned into a pumpkin, I'd go where I was certain no Chicago Bulls Ball Boy had gone before:

To a private meeting in the front office.

Within six months, Chicago Bulls EVP Steve Schanwald was an official Packback angel investor. Beyond the walls of the United Center, the force of energy surrounding the Shark Tank episode was enough to crack open other previously locked doors as well.

Enough, perhaps, to bring life back to the dead.

Turns out, curiosity is a hell of a drug.

Chapter 12

Cage Match of the Giants

One year later. April 6, 2015.

"Dude! That was Mark Cuban," one guy said to the next, as they huddled on the hotel sidewalk wearing their Stanford name badges, "I have a friend who I always say looks like Cuban, but now I *know* he does."

I grabbed my bag from the bell boy. Cuban and I had already touched base in the lobby a few hours earlier. Kasey's flight had just landed. And with the big event finally taking place tomorrow morning, there was no need to linger.

As I stepped into my Uber back to our Airbnb, I overheard one more comment from the Stanford guys:

"You know this conference is big time if he's just walking around like that."

A lot had gone down in a year's time.

We took a brief tour to what felt to me like the top of the world.

I'd never been shinier. Doors opened.

A series of emails and a private meeting with billionaire JB Pritzker. An invitation to a small group lunch with Chicago Mayor Rahm Emmanuel. A visit to Illinois Governor Pat Quinn's downtown office.

When I approached Mark Cuban at a conference, while he was surrounded by people in a crowded room, he recognized me and paused his conversation. "Hey Mike," he said with a smile, "I was just talking about you with Mikey Reinsdorf at our owners' meeting." A little while later at the same event, I found myself standing with Cuban, tag-team pitching the President of Pearson together.[8]

We spent the year subletting office space from ContextMedia, as our mentorship from co-founders Rishi Shah and Shradha Agarwal tightened. Merely a few years older than us, they were the town's true rising stars, and everybody who was anybody in Chicago came over to meet them. By way of being at the right place at the right time, plenty of those folks were then warmly handed over to us. One day, Rishi walked by my desk and introduced me to a friend of his named Justin Ishbia. Real nice guy. After my follow-up meeting at Justin's office, he looped in his younger brother, Mat, who lived somewhere in Michigan, and together they invested in Packback. At the time, I

---

8. I caught Duke Kingster, President of Pearson North America, just before he stepped onto an escalator. After he congratulated me about Shark Tank, I blurted out, in a panicked attempt to keep his attention: "you wanna meet Mark Cuban?" When he obliged, I walked him back to the private room where I knew Cuban's other portfolio company was hosting an event. By the lucky grace of God, Mark just so happened to be wrapping up his post-event meeting. Bingo. So, there I stood with Mark Cuban and Duke Kingster. Cuban pitched. I pitched. Cuban pitched. I pitched some more, and some more, and a little bit more, certain that I was the most impressive thing Mark Cuban had ever witnessed. Afterwards, the two of them took a selfie together. "My wife's gonna love this" remarked Don, as I secretly snapped a picture of them and texted it to Kasey. I was in all my glory. And then, a few days later, Cuban sent me a follow-up note: *When you were pitching him you didn't even notice he wasn't really listening and you weren't listening to him. ...He said he would work to get you in the accelerator. You should have shut up and said thank you. Who should I follow up with? ...Listen more. ...Figure out how to make it easy for Don to help you. ...Those are the steps that matter.*

held no prediction that the Ishbia brothers would one day purchase the Phoenix Suns.

That was just how life went for a few months.

Imagine our parents' pride when Kasey and I alone wound up as the cover photo of *Chicago Crain's Magazine* for its list of *Twenty in their Twenties*.

When you're hot, you're hot.

But nothing trumped the adrenaline of resurrecting a dead whale:

Cengage Learning.

Back in the summer of 2013, we had them committed in a Letter of Intent to participate in the first pilot alongside McGraw-Hill. Then, just as Howard Tullman and a host of other angels teetered on the fence of whether to invest in us, the news hit that Cengage Learning had filed for Chapter 11 bankruptcy. Both of our project champions were out the door. The LOI went up in smoke, and we hadn't gained an inch of traction with anyone at Cengage since.

No matter who I talked to at Cengage, all roads led to a new SVP named Beth Frost, and for the life of me I could never get ahold of her. That was until, days after the episode aired, she replied to an email and congratulated me on the deal. *Whoop there it is!* I immediately asked her to meet up, anywhere, and a week later I was at the Orlando airport sitting down for lunch with Beth Frost.

She agreed to support a pilot and then pointed me towards the two other executives who would need to approve it.

A week or so after that, I flew to Boston to meet with Cengage's Chief Product Officer, Mick Donnely. "Backlist?" said Donnely, upon downing his heartburn meds on which he blamed the stress of working at Cengage, "yea I don't give a shit about the backlist."

A week after that, at the ASU-GSV conference in Arizona, I caught their third and final stakeholder, a Vice President named Lars. He gave his blessing upon hearing out my brief standing pitch that was basically a one-liner:

So look, Beth and Mick already said this is ok…

Shortly thereafter, Cengage officially signed their commitment and approved a sampling of backlist titles for a Fall 2014 pilot. Although McGraw-Hill and Pearson remained elusive,[9] with Cengage on the ticket we were back in business.

And then, by naive accident, I made a powerful new friend.

When I first met Thomas Snyder, President of IVY Tech Community Colleges, I considered his presence and interruptive questions to be something of a nuisance. I'd never heard of IVY Tech, and I certainly had no knowledge that its enrollment of two hundred thousand students across thirty or so campuses in the state of Indiana made it the largest institution of higher education in the country. I was simply trying to pitch his banker friend, John, on making a personal angel investment. It wasn't until I mentioned something about the challenge of securing publisher permissions that the old grandfatherly guy sitting next to John said something that caught my attention and forever changed the dynamic of our hunt:

---

9. Not without moments of hopefulness, of course. During my Boston trip to hunt down Cengage's Chief Product Officer, I also visited an executive at the McGraw-Hill office. A pleasant guy named Stuart. The Boston building was said to be McGraw's startup-esque office, and he walked me over to the Nintendo GameCube that proved it. Before I left, an odd thing happened; Stuart asked *me* to sign something. An autograph for his kids. They were huge Shark Tank fans.

"Well," remarked Tom Snyder, in reference to his firsthand dealings with the CEOs of each of the big three textbook publishers, "we tend to be the eight-hundred-pound-gorilla in the room with them."

Oh.

"IVY Tech" became the two most important words in my arsenal. With Tom Snyder in our corner, and Cuban and other power players at our back, we were hiking to the mountaintop.

Then came an incidental kick in the shins.

Forever in need of more funding, we'd kicked off a formal Series A process. This time, we would graduate from angels and lock in an institutional venture capital firm or two. Solidifying my confidence was the fact that our very own board member, Mark Achler, now had a venture fund.

Knowing that we had an ace in our pocket, but not wanting to be solely dependent on it, Kasey and I started pitching the *other* VCs first, our logic being to build traction before sitting down with Achler and his partner Troy Henikoff at MATH Venture Partners.

As the meetings occurred, and our perceived fundraising traction grew, those other VCs had an uncanny tendency to make the same phone call: to Mark Achler.

They wanted to know how much capital his fund was committing to our round.

Oops.

I felt the pain in his voice when Mark Achler, probably the single nicest guy on our cap table, reached out to inform me that his fund was *not* going to invest. And thus, he had to resign from our board, signaling a fatal red flag to every other VC looking at Packback.

Ah fuck we're toast.

In what became Mark Achler's final board meeting with me, Kasey, and Howard Tullman, the phrase was spoken almost exactly as it had been in our first board meeting with the same duo the year before:

"You *have* to go into survival mode," said Achler.

It wasn't the first time we'd heard that, and it wouldn't be the last.

Adding spice to the recipe, not long after Achler's departure, our Head of Engineering, Martin, was becoming stressed about a product deliverable. At thirty years old, Martin was six years my senior and not shy to remind me of that fact. He and I went to Einstein Bagels to talk things through.

Indeed, Martin had an idea to share.

"Mike," he said, as our fellow patrons of Einstein Bagels carried on spreading cream cheese and sipping coffee, "we need a *real* CEO."

Hire a real CEO. That was the bright idea lobbed my way, by my Head of Engineering, as our company faced its latest fight for survival. I didn't even boast enough pride to argue with him. My rebuttal was simply that we didn't have the budget.

Packback was stuck with me.

Eventually and miraculously, a fundraising lifeline was secured by a group called Hyde Park Angels, and soon we were in our latest investor cat herding exercise to fill out a round that was "angel" by nature yet "institutional" by structure, meaning that all of the funds had to close at once, which meant that people routinely dropped out as the weeks and months piled up in which I couldn't send them the closing docs to secure their verbal commitment.

Then came insult.

Mind pulled in all sorts of directions as the year 2015 approached, I'd slipped on my responsibility to prepare us for the biggest event of the year: the ASU-GSV Education Innovation Summit.

When a guy on the GSV team made it clear to me that Packback would *not* be among the hundreds of other ed-tech startups invited to present in their "venture" showcase, I took it as a personal slight and felt a little stroke of panic. If we didn't make a bang with publishers at the conference, we'd miss our title expansion window for the Fall 2015 semester and thus lose another *year*.

That conference was critical.

So, I went a tad creatively rogue and bluffed to the guy that "we were talking with Mark Cuban about doing something..."

That caught his interest.

It was in fact true that Cuban would be attending the conference, for an on-stage conversation with famed venture capitalist Tim Draper. It was not *yet* true that I'd had any sort of communication with him about doing something with Packback.

Miraculously, within minutes, Cuban answered the long-winded frantic email I blasted off to him right after hanging up with the GSV guy. To see about scheduling availability, he connected me with his assistant, Dawn. Although it didn't look promising given that Mark would be traveling on a string of road games with the Mavericks, Dawn secured us a window of his time at the conference.

Thomas Snyder and Howard Tullman confirmed their availability to join too.

And suddenly, in the form of a fancy digital invitation card, I possessed the shiniest piece of bait I'd ever imagined dangling in this endless game of hunting publisher whales:

Join Mark Cuban, Thomas Snyder, and Packback's Board of Directors for a private Round Table discussion about the future of Higher Education.

The stage was officially set for April 6, 2015.

In the arena of my mind, the attendees were split into two teams: our team, and the collective publishers' team. Also in attendance were two neutral parties: an investment banker named John Adams (Snyder's friend) and an executive at Ingram named Kent Freeman.

Joining Kasey and me on our team were the three biggest names that we'd managed to recruit in Packback's three years of existence:

Our Wizard: Howard Tullman.

Our Shark: Mark Cuban.

And   our   Eight-Hundred-Pound-Gorilla: Thomas Snyder.

The publishers' team roster was equally loaded:

From Cengage, we had Senior Vice President, Beth Frost.

From Pearson, we had two Vice Presidents. In fact, Duke Kingster, the Pearson President whom Cuban and I tag teamed a year prior, had also promised me that he would try to attend after I caught him outside of the bathroom at yet another conference a few weeks earlier.[10] But alas, come game time, The Duke was a no-show.

---

10. By now, that sort of thing had simply become second nature. I even coined an internal terminology for the practice: *Hawkin' and Stalkin'.* Maybe I'd been training for it all along. Seven years served as an NBA ball boy had rendered me competent in the peculiar art of manufacturing serendipitous interactions with important people in odd places. If I could generate small talk with a towel-clad seven-footer getting dressed at his locker, it was nothing for me to hover around a hotel lobby awaiting a khaki-clad publisher executive to return from the bathroom.

And from McGraw-Hill, we had the full trifecta: their new President, Simon Creech, an EVP of Strategy named Lucia, and our old pal from the Kirby regime, Chief Sales Officer Grant Briggs.

Big Wigs from each of the Big Three.

All in one closed-door room.

It'd be enough decision-making muscle to break through our publisher brick wall once and for all. And this time, thanks to some curly-haired bearded dude at Nielsen whom I'd accidentally met and subsequently ate a slice of pizza with, we had the neatly packaged national bookstore Point-of-Sale data to do it right.

If pitching to famous rich people on television was considered a *Shark Tank*, well, then in terms of aiming higher-ed higher-ups and tech mavens at each other, this was a *Cage Match of the Giants*.

"Well thanks everybody for coming out, this is really a great turnout," I said, mouth dry and voice trembly with nerves, while standing at the front of the table next to a TV screen, "the idea here, for the context, was just to gather some of the great relationships and insightful minds that surrounded Packback and get into one room and talk about where things are going on a digital front in higher education."

Attendees nodded along silently, in communal recognition that I was full of crap. Everybody in the room saw the sales pitch coming.

Click.

PowerPoint slides flashed up on the screen.

Colorful charts of book revenue spikes followed by plummets.

Three billion dollars leaving the publishers' pockets for the used-book market.

Doom and gloom.

As portrayed by our charts, the volume of "used book" units sold at campus bookstores surpassed the volume of "new book" units sold by the fifth semester of an edition's release. That was the "window" in which we were requesting the right to rent out e-textbooks for 24-hours at a time.

Mark Cuban cracked the ice by way of an interruption that, in more or less words, instructed me to *slow the fuck down dude*, and then our group discourse began.

Before long, Kasey found his opening to describe Packback's soon-to-be-released Question & Answer tool, which aspired to provide a layer of student-to-student engagement on top of the eTextbook. Perhaps we could leverage it to increase student sell-through rates for the publishers' new products.

"…We're concerned with, 'how can we rapidly increase adoption over the next six months?'" Kasey rhetorically asked the room, "How do we decrease the used book penetration by thirty, fifty, sixty percent by *next* semester?"

Mic drop.

In the barely organized chaos of our curated cage match, there was no moderator and no determined order of speakers, which made what happened next all the more epic.

Before any publisher could pop Kasey's balloon, our Eight-Hundred-Pound Gorilla cleared his throat to speak. Describing his takeaways from the prior year's ASU-GSV conference, the one wherein I accidentally met him while attempting to pitch his banker friend John for an investment, Thomas Snyder gave context to IVY Tech's interest in Packback:

"...we narrowed it down to a dozen companies, and then we gave them a forum to talk to our leadership," he said, in reference to a series of meetings that Jessica Tenuta and I had driven down to Indianapolis to present at, "and this came out as the *number one* opportunity, which is why we wanted to do a test."

I remembered it well. During that leadership forum, Snyder had pulled out a letter written to him by the IVY Tech Student Government, which indeed specified the *number one* problem that the students demanded to see the school's leadership solve: textbook costs.

Had he said nothing else, that alone would've been the best endorsement we'd ever received. But Snyder was only getting warmed up.

He knew better than anyone the challenge of "Withdraw/Fail" (WF) rates that were especially high at community colleges and impacted by a variety of factors, including course material costs.

"...and so, we think that the number of people buying books is measurably smaller." Continued Snyder, "...We've got to get them another option that can get them caught up. And we think this can be really important as far as a retention tool."

Student retention!

The Holy Grail of Ed-Tech blessed association unto Packback by the highest Priest in the room.

President Snyder continued holding court.

After some banter about his dozen or so grandkids, he brought the group dialogue back to the vast population that his institution served across the state of Indiana. In doing so, he dropped the coldest facts in the room:

"...Family income is twenty-two thousand," he said, "...and the book is a decision, that, you know, 'do I pay for childcare, or do I buy a book?' And we think that they're making those tradeoffs all the time."

Nobody in this room of high salaried executives was making tradeoffs like that.

"And they're making them in four-year schools, too," said Mark Cuban.

Shark's turn to bite.

"You look at all of your marginal expenses, and that's what's going to go," said Cuban, "... as someone who has paid for their own college, living without the textbook and trying to figure it out as you go, that's a no-brainer. And you know, that's one of the reasons I like what these guys are doing, because for the W-F students, you're right, every day is a new decision."

Grant Briggs, sensing the direction of the discussion and, perhaps, the rising temperature of his quiet boss, wisely interjected to steer the conversation towards the *other* objectives of his largest client, such as accelerating the learning process with the help of new technology.

"...I have a fundamental point of view," proclaimed the man tasked, in part, with maximizing McGraw-Hill's remaining textbook profit line, "that even if you make textbooks *free*, you would probably see 'digital' move barely, if at all."

He was more interested in the design of the course, and how to drive students away from their unwise tendencies, such as not buying course materials, not studying, and perhaps not even showing up for an exam.

Per Grant, *students will always make sub-optimal decisions.*

Oh, so you blame this on Snyder's students?

Like a pack of wolves, we pounced.

As the discussion carried on, it bounced sporadically in topic yet remained polite in manner. That was until an otherwise perfectly decent guy named Kent Freeman lost his sense of etiquette.

An executive at Ingram, which owned a company called VitalSource, Kent swerved our conversation onto the topic of an innovative new course material purchasing model called "Inclusive Access"[11]. In doing so, he posed a question to the room:

"What's the publisher perspective on that model?" asked Kent.

Ohhh shit.

Kent just said it.

DUDE!

Three years of playing this cat & mouse game had taught me that you never call a publisher a publisher to their face. I'd even specified this code of conduct in a preparatory email to Cuban and Tullman the night before:

**FYI "Publishers" now dislike the term publisher and want to be called "Learning Companies"

Grant Briggs didn't skip a beat.

"Well," he replied to Kent, with the confidence of a jock wearing glasses and a lab coat, "I can't give you the *publisher* perspective because we really don't consider ourselves a publisher. We're a *learning sciences* company."

---

11. Inclusive Access was the shiniest new widget installed on the mouse trap of college costs, in which all course materials (books, software, etc.) were paid for as a line-item on the student's tuition bill, rather than out-of-pocket. In this model, the campus bookstore got their healthy marked-up cut, the publisher got 100% sell-through in the course, the professors avoided student complaints, and the students were broadly none-the-wiser to the costs quietly added to their loan tab.

Mark Cuban's face erupted.

Howard Tullman let out a reactive snort.

Appreciating the sensitivity of the matter, I desperately fought a losing battle to hide my own smirk as everyone not identified by the outside world as a "publisher" cracked into hushed laughter behind Cuban and Tullman's mischievous lead.

Simon Creech remained stone-faced silent.

To his credit, Grant transitioned smoothly into his corporate talking points, under the watchful eyes of both his boss and his number one client, undeterred by the mockery of the celebrity billionaire Shark we'd intentionally placed at his side. He marched forward with his impressive bit, pontificating on about the science of learning and McGraw-Hill's engineering-heavy *cultural obsession* with how the brain works.

The right-hand brawny Sales Chief who'd been molded in the colorful image of Brock Kirby was on his A-game, but eventually his squirrely new boss took a turn. When he finally spoke, his tone matched his facial expression.

"There were *snickers* in the room when Grant mentioned 'learning sciences company,' and I kind of get that, but…"

Simon Creech hadn't cracked a smile since the meeting began, and I hadn't been chided by an authority figure using the word "snickers" since the last time Mrs. Engerski sent me to the hallway in the sixth grade.

Tension was rising.

Creech proceeded into a stump speech of his own, which largely served to belittle the textbook cost issue, and thus Packback's existence, as a small and hardly relevant piece of the grander puzzle. It was the "we just don't care about e-books" wet blanket that ordinarily doused any flame of publisher momentum.

But this was not an ordinary meeting.

"Well," replied Snyder, "we'll find out if we test it."

Simple. Elegant. Authoritative.

Nobody dared argue with the Gorilla.

Beth Frost of Cengage jumped in with the next question.

"Well then how do you see the other side of the coin, which is the faculty, right, and faculty embracing digital—"

Snyder cut her off.

"Well, this group of people that looked at it," he said, referring to the IVY Tech committee that Jessica and I had presented to, "who got all fired up, they know what's really working."

Grant tossed another arrow, something about student success.

Snyder slapped back with a bleak statistic on six-year student loan data.

In a matter of five minutes, our Eight-Hundred-Pound Gorilla was single-handedly punching through the publisher objections that had plagued us for three years.

Throughout the ensuing groupwide pissing contest of one-upping each other with education statistics & factoids, Snyder was king. Aside from being the publishers' largest customer, he was the only attendee whose pedigree included a designation on President Obama's Roundtable of Higher Education Affordability and whose bag of side projects included a book that he'd soon author. The publishers were no chumps; they knew their industry well. But while Grant & co. tossed their impressive array of arrows, Snyder fired bullets.

The conversation continued down a menu of the nation's hot button issues. Student loan debt, college preparedness, graduation rates, something said by Grant about a "fleeting girlfriend," the science of how the brain works, adaptive learning tech, the Obama Administration, the Tennessee Promise, the history of technological evolution. If it had been written about in the *Chronicle of Higher Education* over the past year, somebody in the room was going to boldly step forth to look smart by mentioning their knowledge of it.

All this, just for the green light to let us rent out a digital textbook for five bucks a day.

I marveled at what was happening before my eyes, oblivious to the precious minutes slipping off the clock.

After Mark Cuban popped off a lecture about "the innovator's dilemma," tying it eloquently back to Packback's role as a platform solution befit for this time of industry change, Lucia of McGraw-Hill asked us to elaborate more about our envisioned future.

"...going back to our host," she said, "my question to Michael and to all of you is, in five years' time, if we continue…"

As she spoke, I instinctively leaned forward, champing at the bit to orate my latest performative lecture. Wisely foreseeing the distracting pothole that I was about to step into, the Wizard cut me off on the spot.

"Mike, before you answer that," Tullman interjected, "I think Kasey said before, right now on the table, and I don't know what slide it is but there's a slide, there's a simple ask …Let's test it for six months and if it works, we'll know something concrete, and we can build off of that. And if it doesn't work, it doesn't work, and it's like no shame on you guys. But that's a real concrete thing."

The room broke out in overlapping comments.

"I didn't know you *had* an ask on the table," snarked Simon Creech.

Lucia continued.

"Yea, so that's one ask, and you know, it's a simple one to address. But I think we should…"

Talk some more about the future.

Howard struck back.

"Yea I understand that we can look five years out, and we *may* live that long…" he said, in a subtle nod to Packback's startup mortality as our outstanding fundraise remained unfunded and Mark Achler's former board seat remained vacant.

Our unguided merry-go-round continued dancing in topical circles.

And then, right as Simon Creech was about to land another dismissal of pay-per-day e-textbook rentals by wondering aloud "whether professors would like it or not," John the Banker put his dad hat on.

"As a parent to three college-aged kids I can tell you it varies so widely. It's actually frustrating because they have no idea whether they should buy a book or not, until half the semester's over, and they see their friends try to get by without it," explained John Adams, "…it's a huge variety. Even the same class, the same, you know, 'X 201' by two different professors. *Totally* different experience of what the supplementary materials are going to be."

Exactly!

Preach, John, preach!

It was a beautiful cherry. And before anyone could say anything else, Mark Cuban stopped the show by lobbing an alley-oop pass for me to slam dunk the close.

"Mike, ask 'em specifically," instructed Cuban, "tell 'em whatcha need so they can say 'yes'."

Say two sentences.

Make eye contact with each decision maker.

Halt for silence.

That was all I needed to do. Instead, I fumbled Mark Cuban's assist.

"Yea so, specifically, we are, I mean, the formal request is for titles once they reach this window to be available for pay-per-use, in the 5th semester, and then..."

Rambling goddamn buffoon!

Have you no respect for Ball Boy Commandment Number Two?!

I'd prepared obsessively for this day. Had my talking points down to a tee. Designed the seating chart. Hell, I had a stat about adaptive learning tech's 1963 origin tale in my back pocket that I could've recited without hesitation. And yet, amidst all my prep, I hadn't practiced the *close*.

My pattern of speech slipping out of control, Mark Cuban cut me off. He looked Beth Frost in the eye.

"Beth, would you do it?" he asked.

"Yea, we're doing it," she said.

"Ok we're doing it?" he reconfirmed.

"Yea" she confirmed.

Glorious!

Now shut up.

Watch Mark Cuban line up each publisher.

Let the hot hand take the shots.

That was all I should've done. Instead, I stole the ball back.

In stuffing my own two cents into the margins of his attempt at closing, the bow that Mark Cuban sought to tie was unraveled yet again.

Creech exhaled a final whine, bemoaning our daily rental model's criminal potential for "encouraging cramming." Cuban got lured into side talk about corporate training materials. Kasey explained something about Packback being an "extension of a publisher's sales force that's more friendly in reporting than Amazon."

All the right statements, roaming into all the wrong directions.

Recalling Cuban's sales coaching for me after this same conference a year prior, I attempted to redeem myself.

"What we'd love to walk away with," I declared, voice elevated over the chatter, "is a point of contact to talk about the IVY Tech pilot as well as the general pilot."

Done.

It worked.

Kind of.

I think.

The meeting wrapped up and pleasantries were exchanged as our guests meandered to the exit.

Grant Briggs expressed being "long supportive" of Packback.

Mark Cuban shook my hand and said, "good job Mike."

Beth Frost spoke optimistically about the forward direction.

"Short term we should be fine with IVY Tech," she said, as we talked about the potential for measuring student data in the closed environment.

"Now what do you think about the general 5th semester window?" I asked, in reference to the nearly five thousand Cengage titles we were seeking to make available nationwide.

"I mean, to me, I think it's great, I don't see any issue with it," confirmed Beth, "conceptually I think it's a really smart window."

Fantastic!

Beth parted ways with a cheerful hug.

The Pearson VP duo, having remained mostly quiet during the meeting while their absent boss was seen walking around on a phone call outside, approached me to say their goodbyes. Upon expressing how impressed they were with Mark Cuban, they confirmed that we'd have, at minimum, a standard semester-long national distribution agreement in place within a week.

"So, what do you think of the general 5th semester window?" I asked, in reference to daily rentals.

"I like it, I like it," confirmed Todd, "as the person in charge of distribution, I just have to make sure we're not devaluing our content."

Howard Tullman hung back as we cleaned up. Shaking hands with Kasey and me, he smiled and said, "good job."

It was a proud moment.

We'd galvanized our Gorilla, softened our Whales, and garnered personal praise from both the Wizard and the Shark. My botched-close fumble aside, we'd given it our best shot.

Follow-up calls with the publishers hit the calendars.

The floodgates were on the brink of opening.

Chapter 13

By Those Brave Enough to Question It

"…the problem with our education system," declared Jessica Tenuta, "is that from the moment students enter preschool to the moment they graduate college, they're taught to focus on *answering* questions, *not* asking them. And that's dangerous, because if we teach students that there's only one right answer, then we have to look back at the course of our history and question some of the things we thought were true ourselves…"

That leeches made for good medicine.
The earth revolved around the sun.
Man could never fly.
Women should never vote.

Jessica was heating up now.

Had it been an open mic poetry circle in a hipster Chicago neighborhood, the room would've buzzed with snaps. But it was the daytime crowd at a half-full theater in Normal, Illinois, so heads nodded along silently.

Nothing about her TED Talk had anything to do with textbooks.

It was November 7, 2015. Once again, a lot had changed in half a year's time. She titled her talk:

The World is Changed by Those Brave Enough to Question It

As such, Jessica questioned the academics in her audience.

"...they must instead be focused on teaching their students why and how they should continue learning the subject on their own, *after* they graduate. It's the difference between a zookeeper and a rehabilitator. A zookeeper keeps the animal alive, but caged and dependent. But a rehabilitator prepares that animal to be successful in the wild and then lets them go."

She was challenging professors to loosen up their grip on control and create a "no judgement space for curiosity."

The sales rep in me cringed.

No Jess no! Quit it with that stuff. I'm out here trying to close demos with these people.

The rebel in me pumped a fist and kept listening.

When Jessica shared the news of Packback's new question and answer platform —declaring it a safe place to be curious, and a place for students to become independent critical thinkers—the theater screen lit up with three questions that had been asked in recent weeks by students on Packback:

What kinds of organic compounds would you expect to be present in or around the discovery of water on Mars?

Who is responsible for acknowledging when a dictator has committed an injustice?

Can people with certain disabilities understand what it means to be in love?

The product, at that moment in time, was a janky "beta" wrought with bugs.

But Jessica's vision for it had a fire.

And my ability to sell it required no publisher permissions.

The handcuffs were off. The ball had cracked loose of the rusted chain.

Packback Books was dead.

Good riddance, and cheers to that final slammed door.

It had the incidental effect of letting the delinquents loose in the hallway.

"...you know," continued Jessica, "many professors *talk about* how important curiosity is and how important wonder is, but when it comes down to the grading period, what gets graded? Their questions? And how well they considered the subject matter in their class? How well they dove deeper? How much further they took it? Or, was it how well they did on their exam?

She cemented the point with a punchline dare:

"So, this kind of requires professors to put their money where their mouth is."

Stop it, Jess!

In the six months since our Cage Match of the Giants, the fate of Packback Books played out in much the way that Mr. Wonderful had predicted it to play out.

Snailishly.

Verbal "yea sounds great" confirmations became undecided radio silence.

Cengage's "5th semester window" backlist of 4,700 eligible titles went through the washing machine of some faceless risk committee and, by the time the dryer finished spinning, that list had shrunk to a dismal *sixty-eight* additional titles. Far too few to build a business upon.

That left IVY Tech as our sole point of leverage to prove out daily textbook rentals. And while the Eight-Hundred-Pound Gorilla remained our admirable grandfatherly badass amidst a jungle of corporate wimps, gripping onto his Achilles heel was a Sloth that turned out to have resilient claws: Follett Bookstores.

As IVY Tech's campus bookstore provider, Follett's contract granted them exclusive rights over all physical *and* digital distribution of textbooks at all IVY Tech campuses. The penalty for breaching that exclusivity agreement was said to be *two million dollars*.

Thus established our final whimpering showdown.

Though destined for a stalemate, our ensuing battle with the suits at the helm of Follett took on a momentary gust of momentum thanks to yet another accidental friend I'd discovered at the tail end of 2014.

His name was Chuck Follett.

In the wake of losing Mark Achler on our board, Kasey and I set out to fill the precarious gap with somebody impressive. The first offer went to Rishi Shah, who politely declined due to other commitments. After Rishi, I called up Mark Tebbe. He instantly declined as well, but as was his nature he jumped into brainstorming mode.

"Find someone from Follett or something," said Mark Tebbe.

Then he began flipping through the internet, and within a minute or so he landed upon an attractive name.

"Chuck Follett!" proclaimed Tebbe, in reference to the namesake former CEO of Follett who, now retired, sat on the company's Board of Directors, "That guy's *forgotten* more about the publishers than you've learned in your whole lifetime."

Having sat through a meeting at their headquarters back in 2013, I was eye-rollingly disinterested in having anything to do with anybody at Follett Bookstores. But Mark Tebbe had pointed, and so, like a dog after a tennis ball, I went running.

Got 'em!

Within a month, I found myself way out in the northwest suburbs, seated at an ordinary booth of an old-style diner called Walker's Pancake House, home of "the best thick cut bacon" Chuck had ever had.

This man was different than the others.

In surprising contrast to the smarter-than-you-punk-kids Follett executives we'd previously met, and certainly of warmer disposition than our own ornery campus bookstore manager who'd once issued us a cease and desist letter back when we were students at Illinois State, Chuck Follett was a big, friendly, profanity-prone grizzly bear. Something like a rare Hagrid amidst a campus bookstore industry populated by Severus Snapes. My kind of guy. Breakfast lasted for two hours as a friendship took form.

Despite becoming the third person in a row to turn down my offer to fill our vacant board seat, Chuck took an interest in us. In fact, he went as far as to pen a full-length letter, formally addressed to Follett's leadership team, encouraging them to promptly establish either a partnership with or an investment in Packback.

They promptly ignored him.

Which positively pissed him off.

"I'm gonna light a fire under Don and tell him, get this fuckin' done!" hollered Chuck, in reference to the new company President, while on the phone with me one day.

If only for a fleeting moment, Chuck Follett and I were soul brothers. The old family guard dog and the uninvited new kid knocking at their door; bound together by our shared inability to force anyone at Follett to do anything.

At the conclusion of that same phone call, Chuck dropped the verse that became lore within our Packback team.

"We need to get them to *shit*," said Chuck, "and what I mean by that is, they need to get off the pot."

Alas, it was not meant to be.

In the months and meetings to follow, although I managed to stir up enough of a tantrum to get Thomas Snyder to pound his eight-hundred-pound-chest at them, Follett's leadership team proved themselves too slothy for our startup survival timeline.

The proverbial "shit" was never taken.

By mid-summer 2015, I informed our shareholders that there would be no IVY Tech pilot. Our focus was shifting towards a new product.

"So," concluded Jessica, "the question they should be asking instead, when they wonder 'can I change the world?' is 'why *not* me?'"

The crowd went as wild as a half-filled theater of academics can go.

We were baptized with a new purpose. Inspired to carry on. Jessica had lit the torch of a second company life. A hopeful tomorrow.

But the tunnel she led us down was caked in mud and littered with bones.

Many a startup had died trying to sell their crap into academia.

Chapter 14

Return of the King

2017. The year of the Big Bad Thing.

Two hundred fifty grand! Real revenue!

Can you believe it?

Our company pivot was cemented. I'd survived my subsequent personal crash of 2016, paddled out of the hot water I'd gotten myself into with Mark Cuban, and now here I sat at the helm of a company producing real revenue figures.

Oh, we're big dogs now.

And thus, it was with the confidence of a big dog that I welcomed my former white whale for a visit to discuss a potential role on our board of directors. Following our one-on-one dinner earlier in the week, he'd emailed me to say that he was proud of me, and that I may be on to something this time.

Five years had passed since our fateful first meeting.

Brock Kirby arrived at Packback's office on March 22, 2017.

"Fuuuuck, fuck fuck fuck fuck fuck!" he muttered, self-reflecting in fast tongued repetition while remaining on the phone with me. He'd taken a wrong turn, or something, while navigating towards our South Loop office.

I walked outside to make sure he was ok, and then together we rode the shabby elevator up to the sixth floor.

With ordinary visitors, I toured them around the office, showing them the Curiosity mural that Jessica painted on the south wall, the company values placards on the north wall, so on and so forth before leading them to their seat in the main conference room.

Brock Kirby was not an ordinary visitor.

He led his own tour.

Kirby's self-led tour soon brought us around the corner to a small room with a transparent glass door. Jessica was sitting inside with software engineers Eric Tendian and Davo Hynds. Together, they were conducting a 360-degree performance review meeting.

"...oh yea," I said, posturing as if I was the tour guide, "you remember Jessica Tenuta, our co-founder and Chief Prod—"

"Oh yea yea" said Kirby.

An ordinary patron of polite society might've smiled and offered a tender wave, self-conscious as to not interrupt. Kirby opened the door and walked in.

Jessica paused the group performance review.

After I followed Kirby inside and inserted myself once more for a group introduction, he got down to business.

"So," inquired Kirby of Eric Tendian, "tell me about the culture. What do you like about working here..."

Having completed his unprompted interrogation of our software engineers, Kirby permitted Jessica to continue her meeting and then joined me in the main conference room. I had a product demo loaded up on the TV screen.

He liked what he saw. Ideas began flowing.

"Let's say I'm the CEO of Cengage, which *could* happen," he noted, with a sort of parental downward-tilted head nod and eyebrow raise toward me, "I might want to throw out a question to the whole organization…"

I should admit that my interest in this reunion was more personally driven than it was company relevant. After the Hyde Park Angels round closed in summer 2015, our second ever angel investor, Corey Ferengul, had joined Howard Tullman on our board. We weren't looking for another board member.

Maybe it was closure that I craved.

Or maybe his D-word simply maintained its irresistible magnetic pull on me.

Contributing to my heightened state of confidence was a big hire we'd recently landed, who joined Packback for the purpose of launching an enterprise sales motion. Back in the books days, Adrian Clarke had been my McGraw-Hill inside man. He was different than the others. A young, leather jacket wearing artist at heart, Adrian and I used to meet up from time to time at a little church-turned-Irish-dive-bar called Pepper's Cannister. Seated at the dim lit empty bar, downing rounds of Guinness, Clarke would feed me insider scoops on McGraw-Hill's latest corporate politics. Those scoops painted the map of stakeholders that I'd go hunt down at conferences. In turn, I'd tell him all of the Bulls, Kirby, and Cuban stories I had.

Now, Adrian was one of us; the hire having been celebrated teamwide, called out in investor updates, and spotlighted as evidence of traction in communications with our VC pipeline. Being together in the office every day gave us more time than ever to engage our favorite pastime: swapping Brock Kirby stories.[12]

It was sheer randomness that my reconnection to Kirby fell out of the sky by way of a mutual investor friend. In the email introduction, Kirby acknowledged an uncharacteristic awareness of Packback:

Good hire with Adrian, btw...

Here was the opportunity to put my big-dogness to the test and see how I held up in a meeting with my white whale of old.

After a couple of reschedules, dinner eventually took place at a restaurant out in Kirby's suburb, rather than having, as he originally proposed, "dinner on the piano" at Gibson's Steakhouse on Rush Street; the centerpiece of what some locals refer to as Chicago's Viagra Triangle. Anyways, at dinner, the conversation ebbed and flowed in a manner similar to his original campus visit five years earlier.

Kirby won out as the alpha of our dinner date.

When the waiter arrived, he ordered a double serving of chicken in his salad and openly justified it, "...because I went to the gym *twice* today."

When I mentioned the knee soreness that I was experiencing from long distance running, Kirby warned me to go get it checked out, sharing a story about some guy he'd heard about who died on an airplane from a blood clot after a long run.

"You're welcome," he concluded, before I could even thank him for possibly saving my life.

---

12. As a rising young leader at McGraw-Hill, Adrian was approached at an event one day by Kirby. Kirby looked him in the eye, dead serious, and told him, "*You*. You're going to be the CEO of this company one day." Adrian was stunned. *Me?!* The CEO? What pure adrenaline! He didn't want to brag about it, but, I mean come on he's gotta tell somebody. So, confidentially, he shared it with a colleague. The guy's reaction was totally dull. *What's wrong with this dweeb?!* The dude barely looked up from his beer glass as he replied, "Yea, Kirby told me that too."

When I attempted to assert myself into the role of interviewer, asking him why and how he believed that he could add value on the board of a start-up, Kirby was unrattled.

"Because," he explained, "nobody's done more in education than me. *Nobody*."

Big dog revenue-producing CEO as I might've been, the conversation still managed to veer down the lane of my own career trajectory. Kirby was as complimentary as the day I'd met him, and remained as generous as ever to keep an eye out for me.

"Who knows, maybe one day you'll want a big boy job," he said. "Maybe I'll give you that job."

Alpha though he may be, I seemed to hold something that he wanted. Actively the CEO of a trucking company now, while he waited out an education industry noncomplete, Kirby had been out of the game for some time.

I could still feel the Moby Dicksonian void I was left with when he'd anticlimactically washed ashore back in the fall of 2014.

With the buzz of our Shark Tank appearance still fresh enough to open publisher doors, I caught Kirby and Grant Briggs at a conference called Educause. He had agreed over email to give me ten minutes of his time.

When I arrived at the McGraw-Hill booth, the two of them were laughing with a friend, a former Pearson & Cengage executive turned industry talent broker. The friend got a kick out of McGraw-Hill's employment agreement language, which apparently specified a cap of "one million dollars" on the annual bonuses for sales reps.

"Hey, we're great marketing people!" said Kirby.

"That's *six* zeros" laughed the talent broker, imitating a conversation that Kirby or Grant might have with a sales recruit.

Grant looped me into the fun with an introduction.

"Have you guys met?" he asked, "David, this is Mike Shannon, he's CEO of a Chicago ed-tech company, Packback."

We exchanged hellos and I gave the guy my card.

"Mike, the advice I would give you," continued Grant, "is to keep in touch with David. He's an industry veteran and moves talent all around the industry. You would be considered hot talent after Packback."

The implication was that I may soon be seeking employment elsewhere. When the guy finally got lost, I fired off my latest shot at wooing Brock Kirby.

"You still have ten minutes?" I asked him.

Kirby looked at his wristwatch.

"I have…" he paused, carefully studying the watch, "*five* minutes."

"Ok, really quick then…"

I rambled off a progress report. The student signups on Packbackbooks.com. Our army of two hundred flyer-posting campus ambassadors. The traffic coming to our site (via paid search ads, mostly) seeking the McGraw-Hill books that we didn't have.

He wasn't interested in yet another Packback Books progress report.

To the contrary, he considered it problematic. A potential threat. When I refuted the concern, he elaborated:

"Well look how far you went with just a few titles," said Kirby, "you can tell everybody, 'Look, we already have

McGraw-Hill,' but what they don't know is that I'm just a fuckin' nice guy!"

Grant jumped in.

"Mike, do you know why we're meeting with you today?"

Because you knew I'd find you either way?

"Why?" I asked, with an appreciative smile.

"Because we really like *you*," said Grant.

"Yea haha!" added Kirby, "I fuckin' love this guy! Look at you, standing here with the *President* and the *CSO*..."

Upon reminding me of their esteemed job titles, Kirby extended a bear hug.

"Come here man!"

As he tugged me into his Drew Carey-sized blue sport coat worn over a black V-neck shirt, I eked out a whimpering plea:

"Well help me out man..." I said, while smushed up against his chest.

"You're standing here, battling it out," added Grant, "holding your own trying to survive."

"How old are you?!" asked Kirby.

"Just turned twenty-five last week."

My pitch continued.

Kirby didn't care about the latest pilot data. He was unswayed by my newly signed publisher name drops. When I went in for the angle of helping McGraw-Hill sell more digital books, he brought Jeff Bezos into the mix.

"Our shitty little eCommerce site is doing *double* the digital volume that Amazon is. And that's *Amazon!*"

On the surface, that was a remarkable stat. Until considering what the Amazon customer saw: either pay for a semester-long "digital subscription" at a price set by the publisher or buy the physical, used version of that same book for a fraction of that digital cost.

He continued:

"Look, Mike, I was just over at Amazon, what, Wednesday, meeting with [a big executive]. He's second to Jeff Bezos," explained Kirby. "I said, 'Look, I'd like to do this with you guys but what value are you creating?' He laughed, at first. But I said, 'No, really, what *value* are you creating for our products?'"

At that, Kirby deployed his theater background for a live performance:

"If I woulda said that a year ago, you know what they woulda done?" he asked me.

I provided the expression of curiosity that his bit required.

Impersonating the Amazon executive, Kirby looked at his watch. Tapped the face of it a few times. Took it off. Then held it up to his ear as if listening to a seashell.

"They would have said, 'ok, well, just a matter of days before *you're* fired.' Because they woulda started hammering us on everything. Now, I'm saying, 'what are you gonna do? You're already hammering us!'"

With that, Brock Kirby's five minutes were up.

Seven weeks later, McGraw-Hill announced that he was no longer a part of the company. My white whale had washed ashore.

Now here I was, two and a half years later, sitting across the table from him in a conference room of my own.

Enjoying the moment and flowing with confidence from a VC meeting that seemed to go quite well in the same room the day before, I may have gone a tad overzealous on Kirby.

"So, is this a partnership," I asked, "or is it going to be *King Kirby* coming in…?"

I'm not sure he appreciated that line, but, if only for a moment, I had him on his heels, pitching me.

"Nose in, hands off," was his refrain, *"you're* the CEO. The board should be nose in, hands off."

By the time our meeting wrapped up, we'd gone well over the allotted time scheduled. He drove back to the suburbs, as I remained at Packback for an open mic event hosted out of our office.

Later that evening, as a golden-face-painted hollering improv artist paraded through the audience of twentysomethings boozing in our dim lit office, I felt a vibration in my pocket.

From: Brock Kirby
Subject: Advice

Mike,

A piece of advice for you: be humble - be **grateful** *- and listen.*

Be well.

Brock

Sent from my iPhone

Hmm. My mood, already softened by the come down of the day's caffeinated adrenaline, went glum as sprinkles of guilt entered my mixed bag of emotions.

Maybe I'd taken the verbal sparring too far.
Was the "King Kirby" thing too much?

Maybe he'd truly been "just a fuckin' nice guy" all along, offering me compliments and undeserved moments of his time throughout the years.

Maybe I should have been more grateful.

Worse yet, Kirby may soon become the CEO of Cengage. Capable of a competitive threat. Had I allowed my ego to put Packback in jeopardy?

I thought I'd finally "won" a moment of power dynamic with him.

Instead, Kirby pulled a maneuver that placed me, yet again, straight into checkmate. He aimed my own self-conscious guilt at me.

Reflective thoughts marinated in my head for over an hour as a rotation of amateur poets, singers, and comedians performed in front of me.

I hated the thought of it.

Ungrateful?

Is this what I've become?

Shame on me!

Alas, seated alone in the back corner of the open mic audience, pressing thumbs to iPhone, I bowed down, once again, to kiss the ring of Brock Kirby:

Brock,

Thanks for visiting today. As always I thoroughly enjoyed the conversation. Funny enough, turns out we're just about 5 years exactly to the date since you came down to ISU and hung out with us as students. It's been quite the journey, incredibly humbling, fortunate, and educational, and I truly do appreciate the role you've played in our story thus far. As I hope was apparent, we take our culture, values, and team investments extremely seriously. I appreciate your humility in allowing me to dig in a little as we take the same diligence when thinking through meaningful relationships as well (investors, advisors etc). It could be fun to collaborate more formally.

...PS- the house is rocking tonight. One day we're going to get a live BK piano performance at a Packback open mic night. That'll be success in my book! Take care.

Mike

No reply.

I nudged it a week later with an offer for him to invest in the company, but the reunion was over.

That was the last I'd hear directly from Brock Kirby.

Little did I know, the same could not be said for everybody at Packback.

Chapter 15

~~Survival Mode~~
Winning Time

Four months later. August 14, 2017.

The professor's email arrived at 2:05 PM.

Hey guys,

Sorry for the delay responding. Unfortunately, I have bad news: I don't think I'm going to be able to do a full adoption of Packback this semester.

My stomach dropped as I read the objections he described. A busier summer than expected. No time to make a change before the start of the semester. This, that, and every other lyric of a dreaded old song that everybody who ever sold Packback knew by heart.

Signed commitment forms were as good as Monopoly cards in this game of selling software to faculty. It was forever too early to commit, until the moment it was too late. The best time for a professor to work with us was always *next* semester.

...Again, I continue to be very interested in your technology, as it was demonstrated during our visit last June. So I do hope we can do a test this Fall, and perhaps roll out a fuller adoption in the Spring. Let me know what do you think of this plan.

Cheers!

Our average deal size was a hundred or so students. This Introduction to Economics course, taught inside of a two-story theater building at the University of Illinois, had two thousand students.

20x.

The commitment form had been signed months ago. Our fall revenue forecast depended on it. And the fate of the company depended on achieving that forecast.

Cheers?

What do I think of the plan?

I hate the goddamn plan!

Our hopeful Series A was being assessed on the basis of *this* fall's revenue.

Right fuckin' now dude!

VCs awarded zero points for a "perhaps roll out" six months later.

We were in no position to lose that deal.

"Winning Time" was, after all, merely the lipstick rebranding that I'd stamped on "Survival Mode."

Back in the spring, a couple of weeks after my reunion with Kirby, I'd flown to Europe with an engagement ring in my pocket and three soon-to-arrive VC term sheets in the bag.

By the time I returned home, engaged to Morgan and ready to hire a big-ticket VP of Sales, all three of those VC leads had fallen out of that bag.

One of them eventually took a flyer, investing a hundred grand and articulating the general requirements of what we'd need to achieve in order to get to a two-million-dollar term sheet in the fall. The requirements were twofold:

First, that we hit the fall revenue target that we said we would hit, thus demonstrating the predictability of our core faculty sales revenue stream.

And second, that our nascent Enterprise Sales pipeline proved legitimate.

Our next board meeting occurred a few days after I returned to Chicago. In that meeting, we discussed with Howard Tullman and Corey Ferengul the feedback received from the list of VC rejections, and the looming Cash Zero Date that was a mere eight weeks away. To fill our coffers with enough funding to reach the fall revenue window, we planned to open yet another angel investor bridge round. The board agreed. But in doing so, it was generally understood that this would be our last angel round.

We couldn't keep going back to that well. Angel investors were fatigued of the never ending Packback story.

We *had* to get to a reputable Series A in the fall.

Regrouping after the board meeting, Kasey, Jessica, Nick, and I came to a realization:

We're in Survival Mode.

We further concluded that we ought to rally the team around a transparent shared understanding of the circumstances.

To that end, I scheduled an hour-long five o'clock meeting with our two other non-cofounder leaders: Jake Knapp, Head of Operations, and Adrian Clarke, Head of Enterprise Sales.

Hey team- scheduling a post board meeting discussion wherein we'll go over a financial overview, hiring statuses, and talk through a few operational things over the next 6 months.

In explaining the context of those "operational things," *Survival Mode* was the terminology that rolled off my tongue like second nature.

Adrian opined on a small presentation detail.

"I like it," he said of the general plan, "but *Survival Mode?* Hearing the words *Survival Mode* makes the hair on the back of my neck stand up. And not in a good way."

The guy had just left a decade of corporate stability at McGraw-Hill to join Packback. In doing so, he had an expectation, set by me, that the Series A was right around the corner. Now here I was causing the hair on the back of his neck to stand up.

And if that was his reaction, it would be the reaction of other employees as well.

Adrian was right.

Survival Mode needed a rebrand—something that provided optimism for the destination of the trail, rather than a reminder of its proximity to the cliff.

Sooo… what should we call it then?

Later that week, I was watching a trailer video for ESPN's latest *30 for 30* documentary. It was about Reggie Miller versus the New York Knicks. The video portrayed a basketball bloodbath. Hard fouls. Tough shots. Trash talk.

The trailer was voiced over by NBA coach and analyst, Mark Jackson.

"I remember them looking at Reggie Miller," said Jackson, "*bad man*, what do you have to say now?"

Screen flashed to Reggie Miller. Head down. Sweat on his brow. Nearing defeat.

"...and then all of a sudden," said Jackson, "it happened."

The screen turned all black except for two words in bold white font:

WINNING TIME.

Aha!

That's it!

I fired off a company-wide calendar invitation for a lunchtime meeting set for April 19.

Mike Shannon has invited you to: "Winning Time" Town Hall

Although the presentation dragged everybody through an overstuffed deck consisting of twenty-two slides across four agenda categories, at its heart were two implied messages:

1.) The Series A is not coming, yet.

2.) We'll need to sell our way into continued existence. Like, really sell that shit hard!

We openly displayed the VC rejection emails, reviewed the company financial status, and talked execution strategy. Albeit cushioned by Kasey's show of confidence in raising the angel bridge round required to stay solvent up to the Fall semester, Packback's stark eight-week runway was naked for all to see:

$389k cash in bank.

$150k monthly burn.

Cash Zero Date: June 16, 2017.

As for the product? There's no shiny new features coming right now.

As for sales? Every single rep needs to hit quota anyways.

And then, concluding our casual lunchtime town hall, was a two-line slide that put a cheerful cherry on top of the bowl of poop I'd just portrayed:

Winning Time!!
This is what makes it fun!

At that, I crossed my fingers and hoped that everybody didn't quit on the spot.

"...and then all of a sudden," said Jackson, "it happened."

My calendar filled up.

Dan Dunlap scheduled a Sunday coffee to talk through the strategy of his upcoming week.

Jesse Shapiro, our sales team captain, began coordinating whether he or I would pick up the daily 7:00 AM "Winning Time" bagel sandwiches.

Katy Moore & Nick Sarillo & Kaash Qaderi & Brian Hannig tightened their pipeline deal strategies, hit the phones, and plotted their campus trips.

Then the hungriest dog in our sales fight took pen to paper to write down his own personal version of goals and scheduled a time to meet with me to review them.

The *Winning Time* deal was that I would rip cold calls as an "SDR" for any sales rep who came to the office during the morning 7:00 AM - 8:30 AM and evening 5:00 PM - 7:00 PM hours. We'd hit the East & West coasts during those windows. To the credit of the team, most folks put a few invites on my calendar here and there for either morning or evening slots. It was energizing & gratifying to see their collective buy-in, and personal sacrifice, for *Winning Time*.

Eric Hogenkamp, a young kid still in his first year at Packback, put his name on my calendar for every single morning block and every single evening block of every single day of the week.

But there was a problem.

Hogenkamp still lived out in the burbs with his parents and thus had over an hour-long commute to and from the office.

We devised a solution:

I moved in with Morgan and tossed Eric the keys to my Logan Square attic studio for a week. As a courtesy to my houseguest, I stocked the attic's mini freezer with boxes of frozen Bagel Bites and taquitos to keep him fueled.

Winning Time was on.

Flash forward to August, and after enormous teamwide effort, the goal was within reach.

Then our biggest signed deal dropped dead.

Being twenty times the size of an ordinary deal, the blow would be virtually impossible to recover from.

The first of our Series A-dependent metrics was suddenly in serious jeopardy.

To offset that revenue uncertainty, we'd need a strong boost of continued momentum on the second Series A dependent metric: Enterprise sales pipeline.

The next day, Adrian Clarke asked me to go for a walk.

Strolling down the sidewalk towards our usual coffee shop on Clark Street, Adrian kicked off the conversation:

"Soooo, you remember that conversation we had on the airplane," he said, "about how the twenty-seven-year-old Mike would come out and you'd drink ten beers?"

"Yea?"

"Well, you might want to start now."

Glory be! No way!

The playful little gentlemen's agreement that Adrian was referring to had occurred earlier in the summer, while seated together on a Spirit Airlines flight home from a conference. When I declined the flight attendant's offer for a complimentary "booze ball," Adrian offered up a wager:

When Packback reached a certain point of Enterprise revenue traction, I would "act like a normal twenty-seven-year-old" and drink ten beers with him.

Something amazing must have happened.

"WHAT?!" I remarked, in celebratory surprise, "Really? How? What happened?"

Realizing the misinterpretation, Adrian made a face.

"No," he replied, "I mean …I'm resigning."

Resigning?

Gut punch.

Brain processing.

My mind instinctively shuffled through the five steps of the objection handling framework I'd been lecturing our sales team about:

Encourage… Question… Clarify…

It was no use. I was stunned dull. This was precisely the wrong time to lose our Head of Enterprise Sales.

"Resigning? *Really?* Huh."

"Yea," he responded, "you'll never guess to where."

"Ummm" I thought for a moment, "No. Not *McGraw-Hill?*"

"No no no," he clarified, "not McGraw."

I turned my head inquisitively.

Adrian paused for a moment.

Knewton.

Knewton. The once-darling star of ed-tech.

Second gut punch.

Although Knewton's original founder and his extravagant declarations of the world-changing powers of adaptive learning tech had fallen from grace, the company had recently landed back in the ed-tech press. Its investors found a new CEO to lead its resurgence. An old industry vet looking to get back in the game. Some—or at least one—might say that nobody's done more than him in education. *Nobody*.

The newly appointed CEO of Knewton was Brock Kirby.

We hadn't spoken since his "be grateful" farewell to me five months prior.

Kirby you sonofabitch!

For no good reason beyond heat checking my big dogness, I'd insulted my white whale of old. In turn, he quietly whipped out that big ol' D-word of his and snuck back to smack me in the face with it.

A blow delivered with potentially fatal timing.

Later that week, CFO Nick Currier looked over at me from our side-by-side desks.

"You see Kirby's LinkedIn post?" asked Nick.

I had not.

From Brock Kirby:

Earn-The-Right - Arrogance and complacency are deadly sins for a reason and they are particularly damaging when it comes to losing great people. My teams have always been able to get just about anyone we want to join us. And, it's NOT about being great recruiters. It is about EARNING THE RIGHT to ask people to join our venture/ adventure. Here's how 1) Have a clear vision for people to rally around. 2) Care more deeply about the success and development of others than your own (and earn a public reputation for it) 3) Be more generous (always) than you need to be, especially with your most precious asset, what people want more from you than anything else.....your TIME. 3) Be and do things DIFFERENTLY (ex: sponsor a company-wide "Shark Tank" like event and fund the winner on the spot 4) Provide

*tough feedback - it's what great people want, but you have to earn the
right to give it and being "the boss" does not give you that right (see 1
through 3 above). Good hunting and go get 'em and keep 'em!*

To this day I've never tried cocaine, but I imagine it
feels something like how I felt upon reading those words.

That was all I needed.

Any fatigue I might've been feeling before that moment
was wiped clean. Whether or not, days after completing the
poach of our Head of Enterprise Sales, Kirby's spontaneous
Shark Tank-referencing sermon about his well-earned right
to poach people was intended as a subliminal shot at me,
didn't actually matter.

It was the only interpretation I cared to entertain.

Oh it's like that, huh?

Alright then, motherfucker.

Game on.

As Adrian and I maintained a friendly rapport
throughout his two-week transition period, I gained some
color into how the wooing had unfolded.

Kirby and Grant Briggs, who'd left McGraw-Hill for
the opportunity to once again serve as Kirby's right-hand
man, had gone aggressive on Adrian not long after Kirby
visited Packback. Expensive dinners and sweet whispers of
the fortunes they'd make together so long as Adrian jumped
ship from Packback six months into his tenure (which began,
oh by the way, with a letter of recommendation from Grant).

Adrian described it as an opportunity that he couldn't
pass on, observing several of the individuals whom
he'd most admired at McGraw-Hill also joining Kirby at
Knewton. I couldn't blame him. He'd invested a decade of
his life into gaining status within that tribe, might as well
capitalize on it.

Situational awkwardness aside, his interactions with Kirby remained too juicy for Adrian to keep to himself. In one of them, Kirby reportedly bragged to Adrian about yet another talent poach:

"I just punched Pearson in the nose," Kirby supposedly told Adrian.

Ok, Kirby.

My gloves are coming off too.

Typically, when someone left, we'd host a happy sendoff meeting colored in well wishes, and I'd express how thrilled I was that they were embarking on their next journey.

Keep the team amicable. Maintain calm sentiments.

In this case, I did all of that stuff publicly in our company wide All Hands, and then I tossed the play nice playbook out the window to do something uncharacteristic. After the All Hands, I gathered a group of sales reps into a small room.

"Look, I want to talk about the Adrian thing," I said, voice rising to a tremble as its filter dropped to the floor, "I'm not happy about it. In fact, I think it's *fucking bullshit!*"

Whatever I said after that is now a blur to the memory.

I didn't ordinarily drop F-bombs like that.

But this occasion had crossed a line beyond ordinary. On this occasion, in which my elusive white whale of old had waltzed right into our living room and *hunted us*, the only appropriate lexicon was R-rated.

I unleashed a fury.

Swung an invisible axe that I didn't know I still had to grind with the old-guard textbook publishers. Perhaps it was a culmination of emotions that I'd bottled up throughout the years it took to get here. This was beyond Packback. Beyond Kirby. This was a duel as old as time, manifest into our sales campaign by way of a newfound narrative:

Taking down the "ol' boys."

In practice, we were amateur telemarketers selling a classroom engagement software to college professors.

In spirit, we were rebels at the door punching back at the establishment that posed our demise.

Where are those Shark Tank Spirit Hoods when you need 'em?

Fire in my eyes, I educated the sales team on our history with Kirby. The original campus visit. The ghosted-reply pilot cancellation after I'd introduced him to Mark Cuban. Most colorfully, I told the story of his recent office visit; how he had the gall to step into *this* very room and interrupt Jessica Tenuta, Davo Hynds, and Eric Tendian during a private performance review.

Eyes lit up across from me.

Do as you may to us sales folk, but you don't mess with Jessica Tenuta and Eric Tendian[13] like that.

Adrian hadn't merely left Packback; he'd rejoined the "ol' boys."

And the ol' boys had had their day.

It was our time now.

While a hundred factors could have sunk Packback, a punch from Brock Kirby was not going to be the one. We weren't going down like that.

Heads nodded.

---

13. Nicknamed "The Professor" within Packback for his selfless proclivity to help & educate the rest of us, Eric Tendian was the humble backbone of our engineering team. He was barely eighteen years old when he started with us, looking like a grade school version of Bill Gates. Beloved by all, a few years later he'd be named the youngest honoree of Chicago Crain's *Twenty in their Twenties* edition. But not merely for his work at Packback. You see, Tendian had this odd habit of carrying a radio with him everywhere he went. Seated at his desk, he always had a headphone in one ear, connected to that radio. Between writing lines of code for Packback, he was listening to the Chicago police scanner and then live-tweeting what he heard. *CrimeIsDown* is what he called it. Go ahead, look it up. While he'd sit at his desk, almost always the last to leave the Packback office, over twenty thousand Chicagoans, including numerous journalists, followed Eric Tendian's Twitter account for breaking news and elevated transparency into crime & police activity. You want to know *who watches the Watchmen?* The Professor does.

Fists pounded the table.

"Fuck yea!" replies poured into the explicit-content-warning melting pot that I stirred up inside of that crammed little room in our shabby South Loop office.

Our sales team captain, Jesse Shapiro, couldn't attend the meeting, so I texted him a thematic recap during my train ride home that evening:

The wolves have been awakened.

Overly dramatic? By a longshot.

Did Packback even compete directly with Knewton? Not really.

And whether that little huddle actually touched the motivational chords of our sales reps, God only knows. Rather than a keen leadership move, I'd probably just barely escaped gifting myself an HR mess of my own making. But it was the rally that I needed.

The fight was on. Gloves were off. This was war.

The remaining ticks in the clock of *Winning Time* suddenly took on a newly profane fight song, if only in my own twisted mind:

Fuck the ol' boys.

Days later, Eric Hogenkamp and I drove down to the University of Illinois campus and miraculously rescued the two thousand student Introduction to Economics deal.

Morning and evening coastal cold call blocks continued.

Jessica, Kasey, and a host of others saved a variety of other near-dead deals.

We were doing it.

Winning Time was nearly won.

The Series A dependent revenue goal line was within reach.

And then internal disaster struck.

Chapter 16

When Heroes Vanish and Towers Crumble

September 20, 2017 was going to be a good day.

Morgan and I were moving out of our attic studio and closing on our first home together, a modest condo in Bucktown.

In rare style, I slept in. Awoke with just enough time for a jog before we'd head to the realtor's office. Rolling over, I casually checked my phone just shy of seven AM, to discover an email received ten minutes earlier.

What the …fuck?!

It had been sent to the founders and the Board.

From: *Howard Tullman*
Subject: *Packback*

I was a little surprised to read for the first time in my email about the new Packback financing. I thought the quote from Cuban was very nice. Jessica had mentioned a new term sheet when I introduced her at the CVS thing and said she was going to send it to me but I don't think that ever happened. It's beyond bad governance to have something like this out in public before at least one of the directors has any info about it. Did we even approve the transaction? I've decided to resign effectively immediately from the Board. All the best.

Howard A. TULLMAN
CEO
1871/CEC - CHICAGOLAND Entrepreneurial Center

Huh?

I think I read it seven times.

This was a big misunderstanding. A *terrible* misunderstanding.

Howard had read the recent press release as the announcement of the *actual* Series A.

It was not.

The article was merely the announcement of the previous seed round in which University Ventures invested a hundred thousand dollars. It was central to a PR strategy that Howard himself had ideated at the summer board meeting.

It was *his own* idea! But the confluence of communications mismanagement that led to Howard Tullman's confused implosion was squarely my fault.

We had too many hands touching too many important parts of the wheel.

That's on the CEO.

As we'd later piece together, what happened was: when they saw each other at the "Chicago Venture Summit," in which Howard introduced Jessica as a featured speaker, Jessica told Howard backstage that she would send over an update on the *status* of our *anticipated* term sheet from University Ventures. But then, as noted in Howard's message, she didn't send the email. That's because *I* sent the Board an update about it the next day. Howard didn't read my email. Meanwhile, Kasey had spoken separately to both

Corey Ferengul and Mark Cuban about the press release, angling for a quote from Cuban to make the article splashier.

Nobody gave Howard a heads up that the article was coming out.

And then it landed in his morning newsletter, without a quote from him.

Exactly a year after my bad blunder with Mark Cuban, I'd done it again. I slipped up on tightly managing key shareholder communication. This was worse than bad. It teetered on catastrophic. The departure of a board member had nearly sunk our ability to fundraise in the fall of 2014. And that was with Mark Achler still bestowing praise upon us as entrepreneurs. Now, amidst *unfinished* Series A due diligence, our highest profile Board member had just written cursed words:

"...beyond bad governance"

This had to be reversed. I *had* to get ahold of Howard.

But the Wizard had vanished.

Emails, calls, voicemails, and text messages to Howard went unanswered.

Finally, weeks later, snuck in by his assistant with whom I fortunately had a friendship, I walked into Howard's office one day, unannounced, to deliver a handwritten thank you letter. We shook hands, Howard agreed to resign amicably with an unalarming narrative that aligned logically with his upcoming transition out of the CEO role at 1871, and that was that.

Crisis averted.

But the latest void on our company Board remained.

We needed someone unquestionably credible and whom we could trust. Upon discussing it as co-founders, we landed unanimously on the obvious choice:

Shradha Agarwal, Co-Founder & President of Outcome Health.

With the help of her executive assistant, a friend of ours named Grace Colletta, I landed my call with Shradha Agarwal on Thursday, October 12th.

A few weeks earlier, Outcome Health (formerly ContextMedia), the newly minted Unicorn of Chicago tech, had recently held a press conference for the ribbon cutting ceremony of Outcome Tower, a skyscraper at 515 State Street that would bare their name upon moving in. Kasey, Jessica, and I were invited to stand up at the podium line next to the founders. I stood feet away, in awe of my mentors, as Chicago Mayor Rham Emmanuel declared:

"As goes Outcome Health, so goes the city of Chicago."

That I managed to get any time at all with Shradha Agarwal or Rishi Shah nowadays was a considerable privilege, so I prepared diligently to make best use of the late-morning call with Shradha.

As I was preparing, our CFO Nick Currier, seated to my left, interrupted me.

"Hey, can you take a look at this?" he asked.

Bending my neck to read Nick's monitor, my eyes widened. The newly discovered data point on his monitor caught me off guard.

Is this serious?

The Packback "Sales Campaign Awards" were set to begin in six hours. We had come up short on revenue, and thus I was already navigating a nuanced tone of communication at the conclusion of a not-quite-good-enough *Winning Time*. Now I had to figure out how to bring this latest development—a previously unaccounted for accounting error—to the team.

I'll get to that later.
Stay focused.
Nail the Shradha call first.

When she answered the phone, her voice sounded fatigued.

"Hi Mike," said Shradha, "how are you?"

"I'm good Shradha, I'm good." I replied, "Thanks again for taking a few minutes this morning. How are *you?*"

"Eh," she paused, "it's been a week."

An unusual response from her.

Shradha ordinarily radiated sage optimism & uplifting energy as she sat atop the prized Unicorn of Chicago now backed by the likes of Google Ventures, JB Pritzker, Goldman Sachs, and the widow of Steve Jobs. *I* was the one captaining a troublesome ship. What could *she* be stressed about?

"Yea, ha, I'm sure you're really busy," I said.

With a degree of trepidation, I pivoted to the topic at hand. Tail between my legs, I explained the situation with Howard, rooted in my mishap.

"Yea, Mike," replied Shradha without hesitation, "I know how Howard can be. I get it."

She gets it!

No finger-pointed investigation into my wrongdoings, just a show of support. That was *exactly* why Shradha Agarwal was the perfect board member for us.

Better yet, while she still wanted to further gauge the time commitment and gain a sense for our board camaraderie with the anticipated new investor, she was interested in helping us.

Shradha and I were off the phone before the clock struck eleven-thirty AM.

By two o'clock that afternoon, everything changed.

I received a text from Morgan:

Do you have a subscription to the Wall Street Journal?

She worked at Outcome Health. There was buzz around the office about an article that had just been published. I turned to Nick, and he pulled up WSJ.com on his desk monitor as we both read it:

Outcome, a Hot Tech Startup, Misled Advertisers With Manipulated Information, Sources Say

This wasn't merely an article; it was a bombshell. Although it would be over a year until the eventual criminal trial began, everybody in the Chicago startup community felt the vibrations of the bombshell, and the months-long flurry of subsequent articles that followed it. Outcome Tower was soon cancelled. But I didn't believe the reports of fraud; that highly trained investigative journalist didn't know my mentors like I did.

And at the moment, in light of the data point Nick had shared with me earlier that morning, I had to focus on revising my slide deck for the Packback Sales Campaign Awards that were about to begin.

Four o'clock that same afternoon.

While the campaign had its bright spots, and a momentous celebration for Eric Hogenkamp as the team "model breaker," our goal was missed.

The meeting required nuanced communication.

After some nervous rambling about the campaign target numbers, recognizing the fact that we tried hard and learned a lot, I got to the point.

"...proud of a lot of what we did as a campaign, but we certainly want to have a precedent that, you know, we're a little ticked off that we don't hit a goal, and we've got a chip on our shoulders to move forward," I said to the formerly happy room. "So anyways, that's kind of the reality. That's the situation that we have to take."

I paused.

The team had poured every ounce of effort they had into this, only to be handed a wet blanket ending to what should've been a galvanizing awards ceremony.

"Then," I said with a head tilt, "about ten o'clock this morning, Nick turns over to me and says 'hey, uh, there's actually an error in the way we were pulling the data on the sell-through...'"

Ears perked up. Curious eyebrow-raised expressions faced me in the crowd.

"We're at *thirty* thousand paid students."

The best imaginable type of accounting error.

"We *HIT* our sales goal! *Company-wide.*"

Grumbles broke out as the room processed the new information. Account manager, Billy Walsh, instinctively replied, "shut up." A scattered hodgepodge of "what?" "what?!" "*WHAT?!*" escalated in the milliseconds to follow.

In the two years since company pivot, while traction had grown, we'd never actually hit a sales team goal.

The projector screen on the wall behind me turned black.

Loading...

Nick projected his laptop onto the screen.

The wall behind transformed into a bright white background.

"It just got to thirty thous—" I began to say, but my voice was buried in the eruption. Everybody could read the screen:

Revised Fall Results!!!
30,649 Paid Students
$551,682

Claps. Hollers. Tears.

Austin Augsburger entered the room holding a bottle of champagne.

Packback's office dog, Pepper, started barking uncontrollably, confused, and frightened by the sudden madness.

Team members leapt to their feet. High fives rang out. *Screw the high fives!* People started hugging. Whoops and hollers continued for an extended time as the room remained dark but for the white screen displaying the revised sales results.

Eric Hogenkamp, Jessica, and Kasey embraced.

The bellowing voice of Dan Dunlap—our resident enthusiast—was drowned out for the first time ever, rendered an equal peer to the boisterous uproar.

A newly hired sales rep, Lindsey Cleys, wrapping up her first day at Packback, surely asked herself *what the hell is wrong with these people?*

As the noise settled, I grabbed the yet-to-be-popped champagne bottle. Anne Olson, kindly remembering our last champagne spillage when the large economics course was saved, shouted "no no no, not on the rug!"

I paused.

Within seconds, others chimed in, as if orchestrated in a choir:

"DO IT ON THE RUG! DO IT ON THE RUG! DO IT ON THE RUG!"

Fuck it. Pop.

A fountain of cheap champagne rained down upon our already sub-sanitary office rug. Plastic cups filled up as the bottle was passed around.

A sales rep, Ryan Cashman, was watching the live stream while working remote. He later described the viewing experience with a company-wide Slack message:

…Holy wow. I felt the camera shake. It was white noise after that.

I stepped out of the office to go pick up a few celebratory boxes of Pat's Pizza, a dive spot around the corner on Clark Street. The official entre of Winning Time.

As I walked down the dimly lit hallway towards the stairwell, music erupted from the Packback office. T-Payne & Ludacris flowed triumphantly over a DJ Khalid instrumental.

All I do is WIN WIN WIN no matter what!

Put a bullet in it.

Winning Time was officially won.

We did what we were supposed to do.

Now, like sugar rushed kids at a Chuckee Cheese birthday party, it was time to cash in our winning tickets to claim the top prize up on the top shelf:

Our Series A Term Sheet.

Any day now.

Chapter 17

To the Valley of Down Round Death

November 2017.

I was standing on a corner in London.

Where the fuck is this goddamn lockbox?

The Airbnb instructions said that it was somewhere over by the fence. I was only in town for forty-eight hours, tossing a Hail Mary at a wildcard enterprise deal that had about as much chance of closing as the Bulls had of winning number seven that season.

The lockbox held the key to putting a roof over my head in this foreign territory. Much like my long-awaited Series A term sheet, I couldn't find it.

It was getting dark.

A man looked at me as he walked by.

"Hey mate," he said, "don't stay out here too long."

Befittingly, I'd chosen a dicey corner in London, while anxiously awaiting to see where the dice landed back home across the pond.

I already knew it wouldn't be pretty. Troy had called me a week or so earlier to verbalize the terms. He wasn't so much informing me of them as he was *forewarning* me of them. As the numbers rolled off his tongue, and my heart sank to my asshole, he wrapped up with a question:

"...so, yea," concluded Troy, "I just wanted to give you a call, to see if that would be a *fuck you* hang-up?"

The question itself was something of a courtesy. He and I both knew there were no other options. In London, I was roofless. At the proverbial deal table, I was naked.

At long last, I found the lockbox.

Hours later, lying sleepless on a stiff mattress plopped onto the floor of my rented room, the term sheet arrived.[14]

Upon reading the term sheet, board member Corey Ferengul, who'd mentored us ever since we graduated years ago, ignited our internal discussion with the first comment:

Wow is this bad and one sided. ...They basically eliminate the current investors, knock them down far and then create a preferred dividend that they get, accumulates and is payable upon exit in advance of all other shareholders. I don't see others making much on this deal now and see it as VERY hard to raise more on the future as they control all those decisions. Add to that they create a new BOD structure with them not only having 2 seats, but they have approval over pretty much all business matters — the BOD is basically symbolic, they own the decisions.

And so it began.

The next day, while I sat stuck in transit without cell phone connectivity, a conference call occurred between

---

14. On the subject of the biggest financial decision in company history, stakeholders for which spanned across four co-founders, north of a hundred angel investors, fifty or so employees, a board director, and a company attorney, would you like to guess whether any variance of opinion is about to emerge?

Kasey, Nick, Jessica, our attorney Brian, and Corey. A narrative took form, without me.

In that evolving narrative, our pending Series A investor was tagged with a new phrase that would be echoed several times internally: *The Boogey Man.*

It became something of a rallying cry; one that I wasn't confident enough to argue against and yet wasn't quite convinced of either. As troubling as the situation was, the way I saw it: who's the badder bad guy? The guy who offers rough terms in exchange for a two-million-dollar check or the guy who offers a smiling handshake in exchange for a zero-dollar rejection?

The implied term from our spreadsheet full of other VCs was to send Packback to its death.

So, yea, I wanted the deal.

I wanted to build the company and be done with fundraising. Boogey Man had the bag of operating capital with which to do so. But therein lied another concern with the term sheet:

Who, exactly, do they plan to have run Packback after the investment?

As depicted by our attorney upon dissecting the fine print of the term sheet, my college pals and I could, in theory, simply be fired. Booted from the company we'd spent six years building.

I was torn.

At hand was a bet of judgement on the matter of trust.

As the person who'd spent the most time with Troy, I was disheartened that he'd abandoned the timeline we agreed to and thus hoarded every ounce of available leverage as our absence of any other suitors became nakedly obvious.

At the very least, it made me look bad to my team after I'd confidently declared that Troy was "our guy."

So, I had my frustrations.

But I didn't believe him to be the Boogey Man. And I still sensed that he believed in me as CEO. Besides, multiple local VCs had previously told me that *if* they came up with a term sheet, which none of them did, the terms would be "tough medicine" for the rest of the shareholders. All told, I held little-to-no confidence that a *better* deal was hidden somewhere around the corner.

But it's hard it be at odds with your tribe.

And the tribe was hollering "Boogey Man!"

When I proposed a seven-day communication plan that included me giving Troy a personal call as the next step, our attorney countered by citing the group conference call that I hadn't been able to attend:

...we discussed that even giving the deal a real 'look' would be significant to both negotiating posture with UV and also how the shareholders react. One option we discussed was that you guys respond that the offer is highly distasteful and not a viable deal. You can tell Troy that if he's interested in hearing from us what the necessary changes are, then we can arrange a call between him and your investor director and legal counsel to get a clear read from us about what's necessary to take it forward. I don't think it makes sense for you guys to engage in a back and forth at all with him and if he wants to deal, then he should deal with people who don't need explaining to, but rather to negotiate.

What Brian suggested—offering to have him and Corey take the next call—was a viable negotiation posture. One that, in some ways, elevated my position as CEO.

But that's not how my ego read it.

I didn't like being told that I needed to be spoken for. Something about it didn't sit right with me. An unhealthy spice began to stir in my blood. Perhaps an early indicator of what would soon come to blows on our side of the table.

In the past, I'd gone to my youngest and favorite mentor, Rishi Shah, to talk about stuff like this. During a layover back from London, I opened the Wall Street Journal on my phone to read the latest headline: *Investors Sue Ad Startup Outcome Health for Alleged Fraud.*

Everything about how this yellow brick road of entrepreneurship was supposed to go seemed to be falling apart.

Despite believing that we needed the deal, I conceded.

Under-rested, over-caffeinated, and stuck on an airplane, my grip was beginning to slip on my well-meditated mental composure with which I'd planned to engage the situation. Catching a brief pocket of WiFi, I sent Brian & team my reply.

Then I shut the laptop and closed my eyes.

From: *Mike Shannon*
Subject: *Re: Term Sheet*

Thanks, Brian. Have read through. This very much helped me conceptualize the picture painted of how pieces are being put in place for potential total company takeover ...I like Troy personally, think he and Corey would be a nice combo on the board, ...but nonetheless this tastes increasingly bad.

*...If risk of failure exists in all scenarios, I'd **much** prefer to go down fighting with our purpose-driven team and a high integrity community of aligned shareholders.*

...Jessica had an idea of U. Ventures and this predatory term sheet as a sort of "boogey man" concept. A great thought on whether that can catalyze some of our Chicago community to lean in to this deal with alternative terms, as Kasey has outlined.

It was settled. After yet another fruitless year of Series A fundraising, we were going to shut the door on the single two-million-dollar term sheet held in hand.

When I got home, Nick, Kasey, Jessica and I held a late-night call to discuss the risk factors that we were all agreeing to live with by turning down the term sheet. Nick spun them up into a deck, and I summarized the discussion in a long email.

Per that email, the "Risks incurred by turning down UV" were as follows:

1. Fundraise: inability to raise in spring...

A recognition that, on top of the likelihood that we'll miss our revenue goal in the upcoming spring semester, we've already been turned down by all of the relevant education tech investors for a host of reasons beyond revenue. And even if they came back into play, the valuation may not change months later.

2. Employee turnover (% probability estimate)...

The probability of key employees leaving was deemed high.

3. Fall 2018 growth risk...

The Fall 2018 target would be missed if the necessary sales hires weren't made by March; a hiring timeline we'd miss if the capital wasn't raised right now.

4. Competitive landscape...

We'd lose momentum in the market if we didn't make the planned growth investments into both sales and product, as other classroom engagement tool competitors were emerging.

5. Enterprise freeze...

If we didn't invest in the product, we wouldn't have the ability to take on the Enterprise clients that we were chasing, even if they did close.

All told, it was a robust catalogue of bad situations. Realizing it or not, we'd painted the picture of an unwinnable game.

That Friday, seated in a small conference room surrounded by Nick, Kasey, and Jessica, I made the call to Troy Williams to turn down his two million bucks.

In keeping things amicable with Troy, the blame was pointed elsewhere.

"Hey Troy," I opened, getting quickly to the point after a minute of niceties, "...so look, we were interested because we wanted to work with *you*. But it doesn't appear that your *partners* share the same interest."

Faceless bad guys in the background, convenient for pointing fingers at.

"...This doesn't feel like a partnership," I continued, "we're going to walk away."

Despite the angst that I felt, there was something liberating about saying 'no deal.' We were headed back into a gloomy unfunded abyss, but we'd be walking there on our own terms.

End of story.

I didn't think we were negotiating.

Then, to my surprise, Troy reacted.

Our genuine willingness to walk away from the table produced an inch of leverage in our dynamic. Troy became the pitch man. He expressed his enthusiasm for the business. The product. The *team*. His tone became that of a repentant boyfriend snapped into making an effort to keep the relationship intact.

Though he couldn't budge on the valuation, he wanted to talk about what else might be important to us. That *other* stuff, that had triggered Corey's initial email and convinced our lawyer to convince me that Troy was setting out to fire the founders, was on the table for negotiation.

Among those topics was the treatment of original investors. If we were to complete a deal, existing shareholders like Alan Matthew had to have their principal protected. We *had* to have a path to avoid being a total loss for them.

Troy said he'd think about it.

Internal narrative and sentiments adjusted. After some back and forth between founders, legal, and board member Corey Ferengul, it was concluded that we'd pursue the deal.

But the shareholders still had to approve it.

Back in our early days of chasing after angel checks, our attorney, Brian, had warned me of the challenges we might face down the road with an overly "crowded cap table." I'd felt a version of that challenge in the nerves experienced every time I hit send on the shareholder updates and gazed at the list of names tallying over one hundred people who received it.

Of all the names on that shareholder list, one loomed largest, most powerful, and, thanks to my blunder of a year ago, most precarious:

Mark Cuban.

Chapter 18

The Shark's Uncertain Blessing

You guys took my money and haven't engaged in what, two years?

Mark Cuban was pissed.

Solely to blame, I was scared shitless.

It was the fall of 2016, and I'd blown it.

Three months earlier, on the last week of May, my personal crash began.

With the help of a newfound coach named Michael Balchan, I'd become a productivity machine, downloading new systems of habits and obsessively tracking my time while launching an Open Mic event series out of our office, writing a music project, wearing multiple hats for Packback, and working long hours in pursuit of it all. My time and attention were being poured into every project and person except for the most important one.

We were on the phone north of midnight that evening. Morgan clearly had something on her mind. After a series of incorrect guessing as to what it was, I lobbed up a wildcard:

"Do you want to break up with me?" I asked.

A pause.

"Yes," she replied.

Mind dizzy.

Heart aching.

Systems crashing.

They say you don't know what you've got until it's gone. Well, suddenly the *only* thing I knew or could think about was what I'd lost.

Thus began PGMB: *Project Get Morgan Back.*

Four weeks into it, my journal entry for June 26 included this snippet:

In Founders Forum this week, I said for my 'low' that "my longtime girlfriend broke up with me and the Bulls traded Derrick Rose. So my two main sources of inspiration are currently out of reach."

I was only half-joking.

Months earlier, a new founder had joined our forum and unloaded a sob story about losing his girlfriend. I rolled my eyes. *Get over it, rookie.* The guy never showed up again. Now here I was in the same boat as that poor sunken soul.

The journal entry continued:

…[Another founder] said, sullenly, that he and his girlfriend who he lives with also split up. We shared a fist bump of pain. PGMB ~~Project Get Morgan Back (or earn Morgan back) is in full effect!!

The difference between me and the other guy was Morgan's answer to one of my desperate questions, asked at the tail end of another midnight phone conversation shortly after the initial break-up.

"Fight or flight?" I asked.

"Fight," she sleepily replied.

And so that's what I did.

June.

July.

August.

The summer burned slow as I was stuck in a mental pit that I referred to as "the fire." I couldn't focus on anything outside of *PGMB*.

I didn't touch alcohol or caffeine, for fear they'd have an easy a grip on my fragile mind and hijack my failing battle for sleep. I channeled my fight with "the fire" into exercise. I'd go for increasingly long stretch runs at night, lapping back and forth on Chicago's 606 trail until I reached a state of exhaustion. These mind-clearing evening jogs were soon routinely passing ten miles. The exhaustion is what I relied on to steal a few hours of sleep, before awakening in middle of the night to another agonizing reminder that I'd lost her.

To get through the workday, eyeing my phone for a text back from Morgan, I'd go for long walks and hide out on a bench at the park until my next meeting, many of which I cancelled. On a few occasions, I slept at Kasey and Jessica's house to avoid the claustrophobic gloom of my attic studio. Aware of my own inattention to Packback, I considered stepping down as CEO.

Or maybe leaving altogether.

When the breakup started, I dumped the lion's share of whatever cash I had into two tickets to Croatia on a flight that would depart in late September.

One of the tickets had Morgan's name on it.

At long last, after three agonizing months, the fall breeze arrived.

I had personally grown in necessary ways that I didn't know I was due for.

Morgan joined me on the airplane.

We got back together.

The fire dissipated as I turned twenty-seven years old, born anew. In the meantime, Packback's sales team had self-managed its way to $200,000 fall semester revenue results, compared to $56,000 the entire prior year.

It appeared I had survived my mental crash.

Upon returning home from Croatia, the bill on it came due.

In neglecting what had previously been my diligent approach to investor relations, I had lazily added Mark Cuban to our broad shareholder update list, as opposed to sending him a personalized email as had been our custom when he first invested. On more than one instance, I'd also noticed a "failed delivery" autoreply come back from Cuban's email address when the update was sent.

Eh, whatever. His business development guy will see it and update him.

Wrong again.

It was 2:08 AM on September 20, three years to the date of Kasey and I stepping foot inside of the Shark Tank, when the unexpected email arrived:

From: *Mark Cuban*

Haven't heard from you guys in months

I was in Croatia with my inbox silenced.

It was September 26 by the time I read it.

Shit! I hated to ever be delayed in a response to Cuban by even a few hours, let alone *six days!* I scrambled to type up a reply.

Mark- apologies for delay here. Update attached. ...Can you do a video convo sometime in the next few weeks?

...Attaching an extensive update here on the following:

The attached document was a jam-packed cornucopia of updates detailing revenue progress, unit economic trends, a product roadmap blog post from Jessica, context on our latest pipedream of building a student recruitment business, and a hyperlink to a Wall Street Journal article for some extra reading.

Information overload.

Had Mark Cuban been sipping tea in a library with a few hours to spare, perhaps he'd have had time to get through it all.

But alas, he was not.

From: *Mark Cuban*

You guys have left me so far out of the loop I don't have enough time to try to catch up

Sorry Mike. Have to pass

M

Goosebumps. *Shit! Shit! Shit!* Had I squandered the relationship with our Shark? Had I lost us Mark Cuban?

Sorry Mark, I know that's totally unacceptable. We'll send you briefer regular updates and get you up fully caught up gradually over the next two months...

Another long write-up slammed with information overload.

One minute later:

From: *Mark Cuban*

Wish you the best

If you send updates I will read them. But you guys took my money and haven't engaged in what, two years ?

Face flush. As I sat silently in the middle seat of a table of sales reps actively cold-calling professors, my increasingly nerve-wracking, typo-ridden thread with Mark Cuban silently unfolded. I replied with another long email that detailed the precise dates of the updates that had been sent throughout 2015 and 2016:

…Over the last year, rather than what we should have done in breaking up shorter frequent updates, we sent long-form extensive updates that went out in these months: 4-15, 7-15, 9-15, 11-15, 1-16, 4-16, 6-16. …Totally understand that those are unacceptable breaks of time between updates.

We will continue to send you updates and appreciate your read. This is totally on me, and did not intend to send a message of disengagement. We're working a lot of long hours here and making traction towards bringing you and all shareholders a return for the generous support we very very much appreciate and have been ultra lucky to have.

From: *Mark Cuban*

Your updates were just that. You haven't engaged in any way. Even the round table was just me doing pr

Still a tad edgy from the summer's crash, in a matter of six minutes, I conjured up a three-paragraph counter-debate on which I punched the "send" button without a second thought:

Mark I respectfully disagree...

What followed was a full-length essay that argued my case, before wrapping up on a hopeful note:

...I hope we can work through this misunderstanding by demonstrating to you the hard work and exciting traction being made over here through regular brief updates moving forward.

Probably not a wise idea to poke him into a debate.

Fortunately, Mark let the thread die. Kasey and I proceeded to collaborate on sending him small updates in a bi-weekly frequency. Eventually, Cuban came back, even contributing to a few articles for us. The hot water cooled.

But the regret of my blunder always lingered in my mind.

Now here we were, one year later, and the fate of our company financing depended upon the state of my relationship with our Shark.

A relationship I'd mismanaged.

When we originally worked out the legal details of his investment back in 2013, which included the power to approve or reject subsequent fundraises, our attorney often reminded me that *Mark Cuban giving you a quarter million bucks is like me giving you a nickel.*

Even I could afford to throw away a nickel without losing any sleep. And Mark Cuban, whose tab of fines for arguing with referees at Mavs games tallied in the millions, had sacrificed more money than this to make lesser points. On a whim, he alone could sink the deal.

Before addressing the shareholders at large, we needed to know where Mark Cuban stood.

Kasey had become our Cuban whisperer; the graceful mender of my screw up. We both knew it. So, logically, Kasey offered to send the email himself. But taking a backseat to the Cuban communications didn't feel right to me.

We debated.

Beyond the sense of obligation to face my past sins myself, I felt there was a factor of due diligence at stake. Putting myself in Mark's shoes, a CEO avoiding the personal delivery of bad news wouldn't reflect well on the integrity of the company.

What else is that coward at the helm hiding?

So, I held my ground, and on November 13th, six days since receiving the Series A term sheet, I sent Mark Cuban the rough news:

Hi Mark,

We've received a term sheet from University Ventures for a $2m investment into a $2.5m total round at a $5m pre-money valuation.

To be frank, it's a tough term sheet. At a $5m pre-money valuation after convertible note conversion, you experience substantial dilution.

On the flip side, without an alternative lead for the round, the company's success prospects are at risk. While we have runway through May '18, this fundraising process has lasted since January '17 (Jake's had bi-weekly update calls) and if we don't raise now we'll be missing any meaningful growth opportunities to get ahead of the market until Spring '19.

This is the first of a series of frequent emails we'll send you as we're working to negotiate University Ventures. The intention here is to ensure that you're fully in the loop and that we're sourcing your input as we go through this process. Our challenge that's been tough for us, and would be helpful to talk through with you, is in closing a deal that secures the company while acting on behalf of a range of shareholders. Integrity is our highest priority right now.

What followed was a page long description of the deal terms, our planned approach to negotiation, and a softball offer for Mark to take lead on the round himself as an alternative.

Seventeen minutes later, he replied.

From: *Mark Cuban*

Ask for warrants or options at a higher valuation that we can buy to catch us up

You effectively have no leverage and they know it

M

No leverage.

Truer words were never spoken.

Over the next three days, more back and forth with Mark occurred. Although he'd moved away from the warrants concept, so as not to complicate the paperwork, he hadn't yet clarified whether he would support the deal.

On November 16, I stepped into a dive taco joint on Clark Street; it's free chips & salsa if you dine in for lunch. Seated alone, dipping chip to salsa, I received his conclusion:

From: *Mark Cuban*

Take the new Money

Gives you another ally with lots of skin in the game

Don't focus on the valuation. Focus on the destination

Hallelujah. Mark Cuban wasn't mad at me. He expressed his approval. Hell, it was more than approval. *Encouragement!*

From: *Mike Shannon*

Thanks, Mark. Agreed! Destination mindset. …We really appreciate you being in our corner here. Should have the next term sheet iteration back this week and will send to Daniel/team for review.

Mark concluded the thread with two words:
Crush it.

Chapter 19

Engage All Storms

Two weeks earlier, I'd sent an evening note to Kasey, Jessica, and Nick. There was a mantra that I'd been privately writing in my journal every day for a few weeks. I decided to share it:

Subject: *"Engage the storm"*

Hey guys,

Was just thinking about something. When I launched a new set of personal goals a few weeks back for Oct/Nov/Dec, I wasn't sure what reality would be over the next three months professionally and therefore how to direct a growth goal. I finally rested on:

Strengthen soul, body, & mind to engage all storms

With the recent Troy signal, I'm thinking that ended up being a fitting goal! No word back yet from Troy but it's safe to say whatever happens, we'll be challenged over the next month through this transition with shareholder relations. It's a lot of people that we care about, and who care about us, who are stakeholders in this. Some may not be happy with whatever the final outcome is, and I know that prospective reality weighs heavily on each of us.

Getting to total "forest view", I asked myself "In five years from now, looking back on this period, what do I want to be proud of?" These are the answers that came to mind:

1.) I'm proud to have maintained a composed, objective mental state in my interactions, and reactions, throughout the round closing process.

2.) The core bond of our team, as co-founders, was strengthened by this challenge. We didn't break. We're still a tight-knit trusting unit, changing the world.

3.) With the data presented to me, in a composed mental state, I made fair, kind, decisive decisions and was honestly transparent with the logic that formed them. I can look in the mirror at peace. The result was ultimately the best route for Packback and our many various stakeholders.

...There's no group I'd rather "engage the storm" with than you guys. Just wanted to share that thought. See you tomorrow!

I knew the storm was coming.

I just didn't foresee where it would break me, until it did.

More back and forth occurred amongst the lawyers. More internal discussion and details needed to be worked out. While most of those details were tackled together as a team, there was one particularly hairy bear that I wrestled with alone:

The decision of co-founder equity allocation.

Given that the original pool of common equity shares—already quite diluted by taking capital from a hundred or so angel investors over the years—was about to get diluted down by another eighty percent, a newly formed post-round option pool would serve as management's primary source of future financial reward.

As such, Troy wanted me to propose to him a plan for the option pool allocation that entailed a level of "normal" CEO compensation.

Normal meant more for me, less for the others.

It wasn't because Troy liked me best or considered me a handsome guy with a decent jump shot and the fastest mop in the NBA Eastern Conference, but rather because the VC world operates on formulas. And somewhere in that book of formulas is the potential detrimental phenomenon of an "unmotivated CEO"; a risk mitigated by achieving a certain bar of compensation.

Therefore, part of executing on their investment thesis entailed checking the box on my "normal" compensation structure.

Our co-founder situation was anything but normal.

Beneath the surface of smiley press pieces, there remained fuzzy complications to our origin tale; mostly brushed under the rug, but with a knack for poking their head out in ugly ways on bad days.

Take four college friends and toss them on a project at the start of their twenties; one of them leaves early for a public accounting career and then returns full time a few years later to whip the operation into shape; another one starts out as a contracted employee and then proceeds to kick so much ass that an unplanned portrait of co-foundership emerges organically. The two at center stage don't always get along. Toss in a marriage. Kill the original idea.

Pull off a pivot.

Introduce a severe down round.

The result was a lurking sense of imbalance amongst our core four, felt in varying degrees by each one of us in different ways.

That's a soap opera best kept in the family.

The net of it posed a complicated decision to make. Second only to the looming bad-news shareholder calls, crafting my proposal to Troy regarding co-founder equity gnawed at me above all. I meditated on it, journaled about it, dedicated full-session therapeutic executive coaching conversations to it, went for long jogs and woke in the middle of the night thinking about it. In the end, there was only one scenario that left me at peace:

Balance.

It felt like the right thing to do, sure, but the decision wasn't purely selfless.

As for my own self-interest, if the new equity was to ever be worth anything, we had to execute as a team. This was the moment to hopefully achieve harmony, ending our endless loops of co-founder drama once and for all.

I went back to Troy, not with a soft proposal, but with a deal-dependent decision: my slice of the option pool will be below your "normal" CEO bar, and Jessica's will be the same as mine.

Next topic.

Five days after Cuban gave his blessing, I finally cracked.

It was merely a check-in call.

After several rounds of back-and-forth between legal teams, the details of the deal were finalized. This was simply our procedural Board of Directors walk-through before accepting the term sheet. With Kasey and Jessica unable to join while visiting family in India, Nick and I dialed in from the small glass conference room of the Packback office.

Unexpectedly, the call began on a rough tone.

I hadn't properly set the stage. Corey had other things on his mind. Brian still had his guard up against the other side of the legal table. Our routine check-in swiftly spiraled downhill. A bystander could reasonably have assumed that we were back to walking away from the deal.

The Boogey Man was out of the closet again.

Phone muted, Nick and I looked at each other with a head turn, thinking the same thing.

Shit. This is not going well.

At some point, our attorney, Brian, said something about Troy. Didn't matter what, he was simply doing his job, looking out for us by way of critiquing the other side. It was getting late. I was tired. Yea yea, whatever, this that and a dozen other excuses I could hide behind. The point is that I lost hold of the composure I'd intended to maintain while "engaging all storms."

Maybe I was fed up with being pulled at every angle by somebody smarter than me, boasting an opinion contrary to somebody else, who was *also* smarter than me, telling me to do the opposite.

I was our primary interface with Troy, not anybody else. I'd spent the face time. I was the one who knew him.

They should be asking me what I think, not telling me that I don't know something!

Our attorney was just doing his job.

But I was tired of hearing him do it.

"Every deal, *somebody*'s been the bad guy!" I shot back, cutting him off, "Cuban was the bad guy! HPA were the bad guys! *Especially* HPA!"

I was expressing confidence in my instinct that Troy— like Mark Cuban and the team at Hyde Park Angels before him—would turn out to *not* be a bad guy, despite the sting of the terms being negotiated.

That's not what Corey heard.

Corey, representing HPA on our board and having played a critical role in the lifeline they provided Packback in 2015, heard me say, "HPA were especially bad guys!"

It was a match that lit Corey on fire.

"What? Wha – *what?!?* Hold on Mike! That's the *stupidest* thing you could've said!" fumed Corey, at the launch of a longwinded fiery reprimand that I couldn't defuse until he was done. "…If you want me off your board, I'll leave!"

Fuck.

Corey had never snapped on me before.

Startled, embarrassed, face flushed, my voice regained its softness as I attempted to walk back my sloppy remark. Much to his credit, Brian was unaffected by my barking at him and helped diffuse the situation in my corner.

We ended the call briefly thereafter, in general agreement that we'd gotten whatever we could get out of the negotiation. This was the "pencils down" point on term sheet discourse.

Amicable ending aside, I was shaken. Nick and I rode the elevator down together, last to leave the building as was typical of those evenings.

"Man," I exhaled, voice quivering as the elevator door closed, "*fuck* investors."

It wasn't any individual that I was lashing out at. It was the dynamic.

Stuck between too many conflicting interests.

Beholden to too many bosses.

Later that night.

I was back home in our Logan Square bedroom, phone in hand, having just texted Corey to double down on my apology for the fudged remark. Meanwhile, the co-founders were exchanging messages, discussing something about the final terms of the deal. Kasey, still in India and unaware of the recent tension, said something to the tune of:

"I would have thought we could at least get…"

Whatever it was, he didn't mean anything by it. But Kasey has a way of pushing your buttons. And in the wake of the tense conference call with Corey & Brian, I took offense to his comment.

Another person disappointed in me about another detail.

Mind went up in flames.

Oh fuck off with that shit, Kasey!

It was all too much. VC negotiations. Debates with legal. Co-founder equity allocation. Ongoing struggles with the current sales campaign as the January semester approached. The usual internal grumblings inherent to running a company full of young people. My lack of sleep throughout. All occurring under the looming cloud of the upcoming bad-news shareholder calls.

I felt alone at the center of a knot that I couldn't untangle.

Whichever angle I pulled at, there was somebody to disappoint.

Somebody with money on the line.

Kasey's comment was merely the last straw.

After some unwisely snide reply back to Kasey, I turned and fell backwards onto our bed. Morgan looked at me as I gazed expressionless at the lightbulbs of the ceiling fan.

"You ok?" she asked.

I didn't reply.

Then came the tears.

Chapter 20

Not Supposed to be Here

The tears washed out the angst, and in their wake arrived the first deep, full night of sleep that I'd experienced in a while.

The next day Morgan and I hit the road to Nashville for Thanksgiving with her family. It was somewhere along that southbound highway, buckled into the backseat of a car driven by my father-in-law, radio most likely tuned into something that enjoyed popularity in the 1970s, that I signed the term sheet.

Troy called me to say congratulations.

It was the first of a weekly check-in phone call routine that he and I would maintain for the next six years. The term sheet phase of the fundraise process was complete. Now it was time to approach our final hurdle:

Shareholder vote-of-approval.

The accompanying feeling wasn't entirely novel to me. An advanced strain of an old familiar virus: my countless childhood exam scores that had landed under the waterline of requiring a parental signature.

The damage control routine was always the same. I'd sit quietly in the minivan on the way home from school, blood-red exam marinating in my backpack, scheming up a plausible explanation for mom & dad.

Invariably I'd been "sick" the day of the test. Lost sleep due to all of my hard work studying. Probably shouldn't have even been at school that day, to be honest, but I toughened it out because I *really wanted* to be there for the exam.

My martyrdom established, I'd then depict the upswing:

This is old news anyways. Sure, I got a 57-out-of-100 on this major exam that I need you to sign, but just yesterday I got an 8-out-of-10 on a quiz. Behold the bright future, dad! Let bygones be bygones!

But there always remained one problem: the failed exam still sank the report card average. In a similar vein, a down round was a dilutive cannon ball to shareholder value that couldn't just be erased when the sales numbers picked up. This was permanent damage.

And yet the likely alternative was total destruction.

In the early days of forming our now-crowded cap table, there was a period when I played evening pickup hoops on a weekly basis with an advisor friend who helped us find investors. He'd show up for hoops, whip out a paper check or two signed by the latest angel investor colleague of his, hand it to me, and I'd stash it away in my gym bag while lacing up my sneakers.

It was after one of those pickup runs that the theme of my shareholder anxiety was expressed:

"You know failure isn't an option, right?" he told me as I sat in the back of his Range Rover and he gave me a ride back to wherever I'd parked my bicycle, "Failure is *not* an option."

Until it's the only option.

Upon returning home to Chicago after Thanksgiving, the shareholder phone calls began. Though I'd responded amicably back when Troy initially called me to preview the terms, I couldn't be certain whether the response when I called our investors would, in fact, be a *Fuck You Hang-Up*.

Kasey and I divvied up the list of names.

For coaching on how to approach the communication, I caught up with an old mentor. Mark Achler had seen this before. He provided the template on how to fairly frame the situation:

Dear investors, the business is growing but will need more capital. If we don't add more capital, we will likely go out of business and your investment will go to zero. We've gone out to market, and the market has spoken. We have only one term sheet. These are the terms. With the understanding that the company cannot survive without more capital, our options are twofold: you as the investor base can take the round.[15] Or, we take the term sheet on the table and the dilution that goes along with it.

It sounded simple when Achler said it like that; more complicated when my mind spun with anxiety about it at three o'clock in the morning.

I did a lot of journaling in those days, and the shareholder calls became the main topic of my "daily target" section as I wired my mindset each morning after a long jog and a stretch of meditation.

Today's Target: Begin shareholder outreach to secure company financial foundation.

---

15. Kasey did, in fact, manage to rope in a second term sheet. Not a *real* one, but enough of a decoy to help keep Troy and his partners moving. It came from an angel investor of ours. Motivated by the "boogey man" narrative, he committed a hundred grand, and teamed up with a few of his friends to form a collective three hundred-thousand-dollar commitment to "lead" a round at a higher valuation. ...Procedurally, we first provided *him* with a Word Doc template that he could use, and then he "sent us a term sheet", which I proudly informed Troy that we had received. The only problem was its utter lack of the other $2.2 million bucks needed to fill the round.

By mid-week, thirty-minute scheduled blocks for individual shareholder calls populated my calendar.

Today's Target: _Be present, prepared, & honestly transparent with shareholders._

The narrative was clean. The logic was sound. Mark Cuban and a few other key folks had already approved it. And yet, none of that made the task of pressing the dial button any easier.

My stomach churned with each one.

The conversations started off supportive, teetering on sympathetic.

Hyde Park Angels had their full management team on the call as they expressed the support of their group at large. Something like thirty HPA members had money tied up in Packback.

Another guy, a higher up at a big-time private equity firm, was congratulatory about the "continued liquidity of the business."

Time to call Alan Matthew.

I could still see him leaning forward on that rocking chair all those years ago as I sat next to Kasey on the snow leopard white couch of his living room. I could still hear his pain.

I'm getting fucked. Fucked! Just ...FUCKED!

Now, once again, Alan was about to be struck with dilution, courtesy of his early belief in me. Although we hadn't been in touch as frequently anymore, our relationship had steadily grown over the years. I had come to understand and appreciate this man whom I'd initially experienced as a frightening alien.

Over the years, Alan spotlighted Packback, and me personally, at several on-stage events, speaking of us as a team he was proud to have backed. Kasey and I received unique holiday cards from him each year. One year he sent us a canvas print out of a photo he'd taken at Burning Man. It displayed a goggle-clad team of hooligans riding a ginormous three wheeled solar-powered bicycle into the smack of the desert winds. On the back was a letter from Alan addressed to Mike and Kasey:

...Seeing you work hard and create a company is wonderful. You guys balance out all the con artist bullshit folks I've run across over the years. Thank you, thank you.

I respected Alan, as he did me.

Now here was the phone call that would land me in his doghouse for good.

It was dark outside when I made the call, this time from my own living room. He answered his phone on the first ring. Gulp. I felt the tremble in my own voice as I set the stage, explaining the terms and the dire impact they would have on his investment.

Then I braced for the explosion.

It never came.

Alan didn't even blink.

He was instantly supportive. In his reply, the central word he used was "we." Same tribe, sunshine or rain. His rage had perhaps never been about wins and losses. It was about integrity, a trait that he still apparently identified in me. The original idea we'd pitched him had failed. We'd devolved from being the energetic young cover story of a magazine to tired old news. And now we were about to severely dilute every shareholder on our crowded cap table.

But we still hadn't fucked the Shaman.

That meant something to me.

With each passing phone call, my gratitude journal filled with names and situations. Above all, I was grateful to have Morgan at my side.

By Thursday, I didn't write many words in the journal.

Instead, I drew a picture of a storm cloud. It had a stick figure of me on one side of it, a messy collision in the middle, and the words "break through" on the other side. The mentality was simple:

Just get to the other side of this.

Soon enough, I encountered the turbulence inherent to passing through a storm.

"We were the ones who came in early, and it wasn't even about Packback. I invested in *you*." said one early investor whom I especially admired, "I appreciate this *bullshit* call," he continued, "...Luckily, I didn't invest all my money in Packback, so I'll be fine."

My heart sank.

The next call wasn't any better.

"No way I would approve that. ...That's not even a down round. That's a *re-cap*." He lamented, before diving into a line of inquiry about the business,

"...What's your monthly burn?

"...What's your revenue?

"...You need to fix your cost structure.

"...You should have a million dollars of revenue per head, that's my rule of thumb."

A sense of shame.

Though I felt each one at a personal level, I wasn't angry with any of the cold reactions. The shareholder response was, by and large, far warmer than what I'd anticipated. I just felt bad. But in the experience of making bad-news phone calls to people whom I revered, something in me strengthened.

Growth happened.

Now I wanted nothing more than to engage tunnel vision focus and go execute our way back above the water line. Get our folks their money back.

That became the saving grace in which I found solace: come hell or high water, we'd make the early investors whole again. There was a path to get every shareholder their principal back when this was all said and done.

And *maybe* even a path to make them winners.

At the tail end of 2017, the majority of Packback shareholders voted their approval of the deal.

The structure of the round provided a half-a-million-dollar window of availability for current shareholders to invest at the same price as University Ventures' two-million-dollar check. While a small handful participated, most took a pass, understandably cutting their losses by writing off their investment in Packback.

Soon thereafter, our company bank account balance displayed something odd:

Two commas.

Our updated *Cash-Zero-Date* metric was punted far down the road.

We exhaled.

In March of 2018, Jessica, Nick, Kasey, and I hopped a plane to New York City for the first board meeting of Packback's life after death.

On the other side of the stormy tunnel was light. A new beginning. Something like a post-vomit calm. I'd been through a version of the thing that I feared most: to be a loss for the people who bet on me.

A down round is the kiss of death for a young CEO.

And yet I still woke up the next morning. My pants still went on one leg at a time. The sun came up and I was still standing. Eyeing the next goal on the whiteboard. With a team still intact.

And we all still had more hair on our heads than Mr. Wonderful.

What had felt like falling *under* something, became more like stepping *out of* something. Net of that exchange was a certain sense of freedom. Lightness. Confidence. A fresh perspective mapped out by the scars that paved its way.

The Valley of Down Round Death was behind us. Another log to a campfire story. Yesterday's news. Now here I was, looking out at tomorrow's entrepreneurial road ahead, asking it a simple question:

What can you do to us now?

We're not even supposed to be here.

Epilogue

On November 1, 2018, I lied awake in bed at five o'clock in the morning with a smile on my face. It was a unique sort of smile, proceeded by something else entirely:

Tears.

Once they began, they wouldn't stop.

The stone that broke the dam and opened my river of tears was a one-word text message that my brother Danny had sent me the night before. It was the first thing I saw when I woke up.

Derrick

Danny left it up to me to find the explanation, which took only a few seconds.

Derrick Rose had just scored a career-high fifty points in a Halloween night win for the Tom Thibodeau-coached Minnesota Timberwolves.

NBA Twitter-sphere erupted with roses.

As my mind soaked in the news, I hopped out of bed for my morning jog. Entering the running trail, my smile beamed brighter. Evolved into laughter. Then the floodgates opened to more tears. I was a smiling, laughing, crying lunatic running alone in the darkness of Chicago's 606 trail.

To this day, Morgan likes to remind me that while I boasted a bright smile throughout our wedding day, it was conducted with dry eyes. I never cried.

And yet, two months after our wedding day, I flooded with tears when D-Rose dropped fifty points in a regular season game.

Why?

I don't know, maybe I was just tired. Or maybe the moment signified a long-awaited redemption tied in some lasting way to both my former and current worlds.

Derrick Rose's career was supposed to have been terminated. A spark that flamed out prematurely on that woeful Saturday afternoon of April 28, 2012.

He's holding his knee.

In the eyes of enough naysayers to shatter a spirit, Derrick Rose was the basketball equivalent of an investor write-off. With several more serious injuries depleting his comeback seasons following those 2012 NBA Playoffs, he'd fallen, gotten up, fallen again, and fallen again.

Once marveled at, he became mocked.

After being traded by the Bulls in 2016, he played one season for the Knicks and then wasn't re-signed. He joined the Cavs in 2017, but was traded midseason to the Jazz, who cut him immediately. After that, he was spotted at a junior college somewhere outside of Cleveland with only a basketball and a rebound-assisting ball boy for company, practicing his short-range floaters as the internet laughed.

But sometimes, after the music dies, it comes back to life with a new beat.

Signed by Coach Thibs to Minnesota, he turned a write-off into a new narrative. A once-fairy tale prophecy that was *supposed* to be about a basketball phenom's "six more championships" turned into a story about something more important and widely resonant: the never-die resilience of the kid from Chicago.

Scoring fifty points was symbolic of a grander theme.

Derrick Rose had risen from the ashes.

And that touched my emotions because so had we.

Three weeks later I signed another term sheet. It was exactly a year from the day that the Down Round Series A term sheet had been signed and the bad news phone calls were made.

In need of more capital yet again, Troy Williams spun up the term sheet in a matter of weeks. No drama. No road show or poker game. No spreadsheet of ninety venture capitalists in the "no deal" column. The terms remained at a consistent 5x revenue multiple, and since our revenue had doubled to surpass $2 million in 2018, it valued Packback above ten million pre-money valuation. That brought investors back above the "liquidation stack," thus protecting, at minimum, a return of their principal capital.

The following year, Packback's revenue doubled again, and then again.

In late 2019, about a month after I turned thirty, Jessica, Kasey and Nick were named to the National Forbes "30 Under 30" list for Education.

The year after that, Packback was named to the Inc. 500 list of fastest growing companies in America.

And the year after that, Packback was included as one of Fast Company Magazine's "10 Most Innovative Companies in Education".

In the four years since ~~Survival Mode~~ *Winning Time* marked the achievement of Packback's first near-million-dollar year, we'd climbed up to attain our Series A target of $10 million annual revenue.

Soon it was $15 million and climbing.

With each passing year, the vision set by Jessica Tenuta in 2015 came closer to reality.

While plenty of students infuriated their professors by doing exactly what I would have done—turning their Packback homework assignments into elaborate pieces of creative satire—there were also those who sparked genuine melting pots of academic curiosity.

Although I secretly favored the satire, either way, writing was practiced, and status-quo-challenging questions were asked.

Among the objections that our sales team heard from the professors who turned down our endless cold calls, "losing control over the class dialogue" remained near the top.

I suppose we never did figure out a solution for that one.

But, eventually, even I made my peace with the professors.

Turns out, there's some pretty cool ones out there. And it was with a heap of gratitude that my surviving-founder ears heard more than a few of them take to the internet to say things like this:

This platform has drastically improved the critical thinking of my students over the last 3 years. They are better able to support and communicate their thoughts around a variety of topics dealing with my courses. I teach at both the undergraduate and graduate levels. It has also drastically reduced my grading time for this engagement piece of my course. Every semester students comment on how much they like Packback and found it beneficial, when they thought they would hate it or were frustrated to have to pay extra for it.

Jessica Tenuta can be thanked for that.

Along the way, there was always something going wrong.

But more importantly, there was always something *going*.

We never stopped hiking.

As for my personal pursuit of becoming a *real* CEO, I was bolstered with an infrastructure of systems and support. Bi-monthly board meetings. Every-three-weeks exec coaching sessions with my coach Michael Balchan. Weekly leadership team meetings. A habit loop rooted in exercise, meditation, and journaling. Most importantly, a thick skin and a critical eye forged by the endless debates among our core of four co-founders who'd made it to the other side of the Valley of Down Round Death still together.

In 2021, each of the founders had a first child born: Kane Currier, Tala Gandham, and Logan Shannon. In 2022, Magnolia Currier joined the crew, as did Miles Shannon in 2023, and Indra Gandham in 2025.

Sometime in 2022, as Morgan and I were driving to a wedding in the middle-of-nowhere-Indiana, I passed a highway billboard for IVY Tech Community Colleges; an advertisement intended to recruit students. In doing so, it addressed a pain point that—ten years later-apparently still spoke to the hearts & minds of college students:

WE'RE FREEZING TUITION + TEXTBOOKS ARE FREE

In the summer of 2023, coinciding with the birth of our second son, I stepped out of my role as Packback's CEO.

In doing so, I had the opportunity to pass the baton to a former chemistry teacher named Kelsey Behringer, who'd joined Packback six years prior.

Stable job though it may have evolved into, my time had come.

It was among the strangest accidents of my life that I'd wound up at the helm of a group of people—many of them mission-driven teachers—collaborating with educators to implement a homework tool. Something about the handoff to Kelsey felt natural: the bad student stepping aside for the good teacher to take it from here.

That fall, as planned, the remaining Packback leadership team and its board of directors began the process of selling the company to a new ownership group. It was, by then, our third year in a row of exploring "exit" opportunities.

Having now visited some of our early-stage fundraising tales, I'll leave it to the reader to guess whether there's any drama involved with selling a company.

As the sale process kicked off, with me cheering from the sideline, I texted Kasey around lunchtime on September 20, 2023, to note that ten years had passed since the day we shook Mark Cuban's hand. Kasey's delayed reply, which arrived, characteristically, two minutes before midnight, tied a fitting bow on the decade that had transpired since he and I stepped foot together in the Shark Tank:

What a very strange journey this whole thing has been lol

Six months later, on the exact anniversary of our Shark Tank episode airing, the press release went out.

Packback was acquired.

We were out of the woods. The weight of knowing that so many other people's money was tied up in our venture was suddenly a thing of the past.

Coincidentally, on the evening of the same day that the deal closed, I was scheduled to present a brief update to the members of Hyde Park Angels in Chicago.

"Well, this is kinda weird to say," I opened, "Packback sold this morning."

As for the final score: while it was the post-pivot investors who did best, nobody lost a dollar on Packback. And, given their participation across multiple rounds, when HPA's Managing Director Pete Wilkins presented the members with an update on the overall portfolio returns as I sat in attendance watching, there it was: the quadrant of exited portfolio companies deemed return-on-investment "winners."

Packback had, by the skin of our teeth, made it in.

Now I could officially say it: *Winning Time was won.*

To celebrate, the next day at lunch Morgan and I went to Chipotle, ordered two burritos to-go, stuffed them into our coat pockets, and snuck 'em into an empty movie theatre to watch a flick while the kids were at daycare.

It's the little things in life.

On the Monday following my last official Friday employed at Packback, I went to work on starting a new company.

In catching up with a few old acquaintances, there was a hint of déjà vu in the air. The first milestone I wrote down was a familiar one:

Mark Achler said good idea!

Mark Cuban wished me good luck.

And the most active respondent of the first network update was a familiar voice as well: Howard Tullman went out of his way to help.

As far as I can tell, no matter the heat of yesterday's flame, a bridge can always be repaired. Or rebuilt.

Around the same time, I paid a long overdue visit to our Shaman.

Alan Matthew and I shared a round of cigars on the balcony of his high rise, swapping stories and peering out over Lake Michigan as I pointed at the boats on which I'd worked as a deckhand so many years earlier during the summers between ball boy seasons.

Aside from the piles of printed Burning Man photos that covered his white marble floor as he was organizing & donating his extensive collection, the décor of Alan's condo remained about the same: the waterfall in the entryway, the wall of imported woodwork as a backdrop to the statues of goddesses, the aroma of incense, and that same snow leopard white couch on which Kasey and I had sat to pitch our first investor over ten years before.

In that regard, not much had changed.

But Alan had.

There was a levity to the once-strange man I'd so feared that I might wrong if Packback failed, but who somehow hadn't blinked when it did. Same ponytail, but rather than slick black, his hair was a mixture of white and grey. It suited him better, I thought, wasn't colored anything other than what it was.

He wore a T-shirt that read, *Church of the Open Mind.*

Having recently entered his seventies, I asked him a question about his thoughts on the future. At that, Alan went quiet for an extended moment as he stared off at the water's horizon. We both embraced the silence. And then a subtle smile cracked his lips as he tilted his head and replied:

"I'm so *fuckin'* bullish."

Having dabbled back in his old trading domain, Alan was bullish about the markets. But more than that, he was bullish about the world.

Bullish about life.

Come to think of it, so am I.

Go Bulls.

Gratitude

The process of writing this book sent me down a long arduous tunnel that, at times, I feared I would never find my way out of. It was in the Spring of 2020 that I first took a stab at organizing something like six hundred pages of assorted journal entries that I'd written throughout a ten-year period, capturing the scenes, quotes, and details of this story as they occurred. Naively, I estimated that I'd have that mound of notes transformed into a book in about six months, maybe a year. Five years and over a thousand hours logged in Dark AM writing & editing sessions later, here we are.

I provide that context as the backdrop for appreciating, first and foremost, my wife Morgan. What a strange (annoying?) thing it must have been to be married to an obsessed lunatic who spent so much time alone at odd hours in a candlelit room with the door closed, working on something that nobody else knew about but you. You were never less than fully patient with me and provided the lifeline spark of encouragement whenever I was stuck. The same could be said of your role throughout the rest of our life journey together. You're my best bud, and perennial Mom of the Year for our boys. I love you. Thank you, Morgan.

To my editor and de facto writing coach, Andrew McFadyen-Ketchum. By the time I reluctantly gave in to Morgan's advice to engage a professional editor, I was four years deep in the process, polishing off the fifth draft of my monolithic self-edited manuscript. I had "trimmed" it down to 434 pages and considered it complete. Handing it to an editor would simply be a check-the-box exercise, I thought. And then Andrew did the thing that I had dreaded most about engaging an editor: he thoughtfully articulated why my manuscript was far too long and how it might benefit from a complete narrative restructuring. Gulp. *Screw this guy!* I went for a walk. Slept on it. Considered tossing the whole thing in the trash. And then I finally arrived at the conclusion that Andrew was right. *Advance the narrative.* Thank you for the gentle guidance, sir. We got it done.

To my Packback co-founders, Nick Currier, Jessica Tenuta, and Kasey Gandham. How lucky was I to ride each of your coattails and spend a decade doing cool things with my best friends. Thanks for believing in this curly haired schmuck back in the day, and for not giving up on me as I grew. You're stuck with me now, suckers. Family's family.

Speaking of luck, among the luckiest days of my life was the day when my old pals Brendan Ryan and Pat Reardon pinged me about a Chicago Bulls team scrimmage as the 2007 NBA season kicked off. Kevin D had chosen you guys, not me. But then Brendan Ryan boldly and generously sent the most artfully crafted email in the history of seventeen-year-olds to Bulls Trainer Marc Boff, and by some miracle the doors to Gate Three-and-a-Half cracked open for me. I'll never forget that. Rough tough real stuff, my guys.

Something of an academic black sheep, it's no secret that I wasn't much for schoolwork as a kid, and I remain a skeptic of academia's design. Nonetheless, there are those teachers out there who manage, heroically, to make their indelible mark even on us class clowns. My sophomore year high school English teacher, Ms. Rosaleen Behnken, stands out above all as the good teacher who knocked over the early dominos that led to my formation as an author. She used to assign these ordinary, one- or two-page essays. In turn, I'd routinely transform the assignment into a piece of ludicrous satire, certain that my nonsense would land me in trouble and yet too consumed in genuine creative flow to get my pen to behave properly. Ms. Behnken never scolded my literary malfeasance. Instead, she'd have a laugh, tack on a few extra credit points, pull me aside for words of encouragement, and on several occasions requested of me to read my absurd little essays to the rest of the class. In a sense, Ms. Behnken granted me the license to write on instinct, rather than on academic spec. I had similar experiences with Mr. Peter Gallo in high school, and Professor Joe Solberg in college. Thank you all.

In terms of developing an entrepreneurial skillset, the practice doesn't begin only after you've launched a company. It starts with all of those summer gigs, side hustles, and odd jobs performed throughout life. And if a young kid gets their first shot at managing any sort of operation, the entrepreneurial learning curve accelerates unknowingly. In my case, that shift occurred at age eighteen, as the youngest "dock manager" working for a Chicago River boat touring company called Chicago Line Cruises. For that, I owe a debt of gratitude to the likes of Terry Johnson, Vince Voss, Roc

"Puma" O'Connor (RIP), and of course the incomparable Captain Dick Dalton who – for better or worse depending on who you ask – may have incidentally shaped my pen's vernacular. Code Blue, Captain.

The world of the NBA was, in my eyes, the ultimate surreal fantasy land to be a part of. Thank you to Marc Boff for hiring me to the Bulls, to Jeff Tanaka for your lasting friendship and for keeping me in your rotation throughout the seasons when my availability narrowed to weekends-only, to Bulls assistant coach Mike Wilhelm for being my early mentor and champion, and to Mike Smetana, who alongside Kevin D'Agostino and the legendary O'Neil brothers gave me the vet's stamp of approval inside of Ball Boy Land. Those Bulls days were a dream come true. To that end, when Jeff Tanaka invited me to volunteer at my first NBA Draft Combine, the door to another fantasy world was unlocked: Attack Athletics, the kingdom of Tim Grover. While many of the cherished stories that I'd written from that summer have been edited out of this final book draft, our summer together left yet another indelible mark that shaped me for years to come. Thank you to Tim Grover, Mike Procopio, Matt Alarcon, Joe Boylan, Malcolm Price, Jonathon James, Yusuke Nakayama, and Norm DeSilva. Y'all were, to put it in your language, *some tough motherfuckers*; it was an honor to serve the rare environment that you cultivated. To my Attack peers, while I took a left turn out of the path that we were all pursuing, you know that I'm always rooting you on and still expertly stirring the Gatorade over here on the sidelines as you climb: August Mendez, Matt Cline, George Galanopoulos, Franklin Griffin, Danny Boylan, Elias Boyer, & DeAngelo Shears.

Thank you to all of my fellow Packbackers. There's far too many to name, and I'd be horrified to miss someone, so I'll leave it at this. You know who you are. Thank you. We did it together, and the *Packsack Alumni Mafia* lives on forever. We'll always be a team, and I'm always a phone call away.

Thank you to Michael Balchan, my personal coach and sherpa who shaped my self-systems and walked with me throughout the tough times. When Rich Woo first introduced us, I pitched you to be an angel investor. Instead, you simply stepped into the role of behind-the-scenes angel for a flailing entrepreneur & writer. I'll never know why you took an interest in my development, but I'm sure grateful that you did. Thanks, coach. Thank you to Alan Matthew, for making the first bet, and for standing by the tribe through thick and thin.

Thank you to Corey Ferengul, who was there with us at the very beginning by writing a an early check along with Alan Matthew and Leo Shapiro, and was still right there with us eleven years later throughout the exit process. Who could have ever predicted the marathon that we were dragging you into? Thanks for never losing the faith, and for always answering the phone. Go Redbirds.

Thank you to Mark Achler and Howard Tullman, who gave us our first stamp of credibility, and shaped us into the founders we needed to become. I'll never forget my one-on-one coaching sessions with Mark as I aspired to become a "real CEO", and I can still feel the adrenaline of waking up at 4:30 AM to send "Tullman Time" email updates to Howard. You guys opened the door to Chicago and set us on the course to become entrepreneurs within your playground. Thank you both.

Thank you to Mark Cuban for going against the current of his fellow Sharks by taking an interest in two young first-time entrepreneurs with a mere $120 dollars in revenue. The question that everybody asks of anybody who lands on Shark Tank is, "what's the Shark like after the show?" Mark Cuban is, simply put, authentic. He rolled up his sleeves, he gave us his time, replied instantly to emails, and was the exact same down-to-earth person behind the scenes as he was on the TV screen. Thank you, Mark, for believing in me, for the occasional tough love, and for sticking with me through my stumbles. Oh, and thanks for sticking to our original terms after Kasey's infamous reverse math blooper too.

Thank you to Steve Schanwald, for taking an interest in the oddly mysterious "ball boy on Shark Tank," and inviting me to perhaps the only place where no ball boy had gone before: to a meeting with a top executive in the Chicago Bulls front office. I've cherished our lasting friendship that lives on because of that meeting. Thanks for betting on me, Steve.

Thank you to Troy Williams, for believing in me and making the substantive investment that solidified Packback's second life. Designing a proper financing round on a pivoted company with a legacy cap table is a tricky thing. What was feared at the time as the *Big Bad Thing* proved itself to be the *Big Right Step* forward, constructed on logical & fair terms. I appreciated our weekly phone calls, board camaraderie, and positive relationship throughout six years working together.

Thank you to anyone at any of the textbook publishers who ever answered a cold call from me, responded to an email, or lent me your time at a conference. I appreciate you. In the grand narrative of the "college kids trying to disrupt textbook costs", a headline magnified (much to my strategic enjoyment) by Mr. Wonderful on national television, the textbook publishers were naturally cast as the collective antagonist. But within the big clunky machine, these were, by and large, good people. Family folks like any of the rest of us, just doing their jobs. Higher education is an ecosystem that lends itself to unnatural economics. The vast majority of these folks weren't responsible for designing the structures that proliferated the infamous textbook price inflation that we were rallying against. The knot is far more entangled than that. I appreciate you all for hearing us out and in turn becoming a part of my story. I wish you all the best.

Thank you to all of the college professors who gave Packback's second life a chance at survival, and stuck with us. Folks like Doan Winkel, Brandon Chicotsky, Jodee Halsten, Jose Vazquez, Barbara Ribbens, and so many others over the years. You didn't have to try out a no-brand new tool, but you gave us a shot and in turn gave us a little bit of extra life. To that end, I owe an extra special call out to my dear old friend Professor Leslie Hendon of University of Alabama at Birmingham, whose "dolphin leaps of joy" enthusiasm injected the energy in us to get over the hurdles in more ways than you know. Leslie, your colorful jersey hangs in our rafters for eternity. Thank you all.

Thank you to anyone who ever opened a "friends of Packback" network and/or investor update email. Good folks like Professor Terry Lowe, Anthony Knierim, Rick

Desai, Kelsey Lutz, Jeff Cantalupo, Nick Begich, Devin Johnson, Sam Guren, Mike Gamson, Owen & Leo J. Shapiro (RIP), Mathew Smith, Brian Axelrad, Bailey Moore, Mark Tebbe, Elle & Tim Bruno, Corey Maggette, Jason Komosa, Andrew & Tom Feichter, Bob Fix, Ryan DeVore, Phil Reitz, Justin & Mat Ishbia, Michael Tanney, Ron Levin, Pete Wilkins, Michael Sachaj, Dan Korybalski, Joe LaManna, Rishi & Shradha, George Bousis, Rich Woo, Tom Sosnoff, Matt Saverin, Brad Serot, Nathan Matthews, Eric Meizlish, Patrick Daley, Matt Raino, Dan & Taryn Aronson, Maurice Cheeks, Chad Moser, Derek Vogler, John Endlund, Mark Burns, David Mann, Jon McCulloch, Dudley Beyler, Jamie Caras, Jori Pearsall, Shu Duan, Chris Bobowski, David Roland, Cassidy Leventhal & Lauren Goldman and the team at University Ventures, Raaja Nemani, Bernie Dan, Larry Wert, Brad Aubuchon, Kevin Toller, Zain Raj, John Adams, Jason Conrad, Tyler Ward, Sam McIngvale, Rob Topping, Cayce Stone, Andy Tong, Nathan Parker, Dave Petersen, Jacob Phillips, Arpan Patel & the team at MD Angels, Dan Barotz, Doug Gessner, Lori Healey, Phil Kim & Mayra Lombera and the team at 20 Million Minds, Ajay Pattani, Bob Shah, Jake Poliskin, Stephen Feldman, John Bintz, Mark Ament, Anthony Cordano, Chris D'Cruz, Vincent Luan, Sanjiv Patel, Alan Rheingold, Rafael Tohme, Philip Wilson, Ellis & Jan Augsburger, Eric Green, David Johnson, John Lawrence, Christian Sullivan, Ryan Feit, Aaron Kellner, and so many others who spent so many hours lending a hand. There are enough folks deserving of multi-paragraph gratitude that I could spend another twenty or so pages on this section. With apologies for the brevity and for any folks who I may have missed, I'd like to simply say thank you.

A final and special thank you to my friend Matt Vari, a creative partner in arms who rolled up his operational sleeves with me to ensure that this book found its way into the world.

Onward & upwards.

Mike

www.ingramcontent.com/pod-product-compliance
Lightning Source LLC
Chambersburg PA
CBHW030913120626
46554CB00001B/135

9 7 9 8 9 9 8 8 9 2 0 0 4